To
Ron & Iris

From
MaryAnn

03/17/03

TRIUMPH
OVER TRAGEDY

TRIUMPH
OVER TRAGEDY

SEPTEMBER 11 AND THE REBIRTH OF A BUSINESS

JOHN DUFFY

CHAIRMAN AND CEO, KEEFE, BRUYETTE & WOODS

and MARY S. SCHAEFFER

WITH CONTRIBUTIONS FROM THE EMPLOYEES OF KBW

JOHN WILEY & SONS, INC.

All KBW royalties from the sale of this
book will go to the KBW Family Fund.

For general information on our other products and services, or technical support,
please contact our Customer Care Department within the United States at
800–762-2974, outside the United States at 317–572-3993 or fax 317–572-4002.

Wiley also publishes its books in a variety of electronic formats. Some content that
appears in print may not be available in electronic books.

ISBN: 0-471-24438-4

Printed in the United States of America.

10 9 8 7 6 5 4 3 2 1

For my son Christopher
and
the 66 other employees we lost on 9/11

They Sped Too Soon

They sped too soon
To a province we didn't know existed
Yet, it always has been and always will be
Is it eternal, everlasting.

For that we must wait.
We are bound in grief
Our province has a border of despair
Yet the memories of joy are deeply woven.

In their province their souls
Reach their natural fullness
How pure can the light be
Is it such that it leaves only love.

A. M. Senchak

ACKNOWLEDGMENTS

I cannot say enough about what the Keefe, Bruyette & Woods employees have done in the last six months. In addition to helping rebuild our firm and assist the families of the people we lost, many have been extraordinarily generous in the time they devoted to this project. Approximately 30 of our folks sat for interviews that resulted in over 600 pages of commentary for this book. For many, talking about what happened was difficult but they insisted on doing it. A few were either still too shaken to talk or were so busy trying to get us up and running again that they simply were not available. This book is a tribute to the spirit and determination of all the fine people who have worked so hard to make our firm the shining star that it is and I thank them.

I would be remiss if I did not add a special thanks to our editor Jeanne Glasser and the folks at John Wiley & Sons for their outstanding efforts and compassionate understanding of our special circumstances.

CONTENTS

PROLOGUE

O n the morning of September 11, 2001, a bright and beautiful day, I was co-CEO and president of Keefe, Bruyette & Woods, Inc. (KBW), a boutique investment banking and brokerage firm. We had fully recovered from a scandal two years earlier—one that had rocked our firm to the very roots of its foundation—and had moved into a handsome new office space on the 88th and 89th floor in the World Trade Center. We were on track for a banner year and were contemplating a merger with a prestigious French bank. Within our industry, we were known and well respected for our research efforts.

When I left my Westchester home around 8 A.M. to head for the office, life was good. Within the next three hours, I learned that I lost my son who was an employee of KBW; my co-CEO, a man I had worked closely with for many years; 65 other associates; our corporate headquarters; and all of our documents. This is the story of how, with the help of family, friends, associates, and the generosity of some of our competitors, we succeeded in taking care of our surviving employees, assisting the families of those we had lost, and rebuilding our company.

PART I

TRAGEDY

LIFE BEFORE 9/11

Keefe, Bruyette & Woods (KBW) is a Wall Street firm specializing in the banking, insurance, and financial services industries. Our corporate culture differs from many Wall Street firms. KBW has very low turnover, often people stay at KBW for 20 or more years. While our obligations to our clients have been a priority, we never forget the needs of our own employees.

September 11, 2001, was particularly painful for many of us when we lost not only employees, but employees who had become close friends—who were like family.

There is a great deal of variation in what KBW does. We're known for our research and pride ourselves on having the best analysts in the areas we cover. Although KBW has long been recognized as a banking industry authority, in recent years, we've expanded our focus to include insurance companies, broker/dealers, mortgage banks, asset-management companies, and specialty finance firms.

In the World Trade Center, we occupied the 88th and 89th floors of the South Tower. Our corporate finance and investment bankers were housed on the 88th floor and our research analysts and traders were on the 89th floor.

A typical day at KBW began when the first employees arrived on the 89th floor a little after 7 A.M. to prepare for our morning meeting. The meeting generally began between 7:30 and 7:45 with our research people, traders, and salespeople in attendance. Although it is hosted in New York, our regional offices in Hartford, Boston, Columbus, and San Francisco attend via telephone. At the meeting, our research analysts share the latest news, analyses, and related information about the companies that they cover with the traders and salespeople.

The information presented is augmented throughout the day as the analysts uncover additional data that might help the traders and salespeople do their jobs. Not all of the analysts attend each meeting since some of them might be traveling to visit clients, attending conferences, or taking personal time.

After the meeting, which generally lasts from 30 to 45 minutes, the traders and salespeople return to their desks and begin to share information with their contacts via telephone and e-mail. They spend the rest of the day talking with clients, with the salespeople taking orders and the traders executing those orders. The traders' day ends around 4:30 P.M., while the salespeople leave half an hour to an hour later. Since most days start before 7:30 A.M., and often include working lunches and/or working dinners, our employees put in long hours.

Research is the heart of Keefe, Bruyette & Woods. It is what we are known for and the key to the value we bring to our brokerage customers. The integrity of KBW's research enables the firm to build strong relationships with scores of companies. It also gives us the critical perspective we need to work with our corporate finance clients. We have been consistently named the "Best of the Boutiques" for money-center and regional bank research in *Institutional Investor's* annual All American Research Team Poll.

In 2001, we won the title in five areas: Multinational Banks, Regional Banks, Brokers & Asset Managers, Mortgage Finance, and Specialty Finance. Our professionals follow close to 400 financial services companies—more than any other brokerage firm. *KBW's Action List,* our research department's report of the best investment ideas, has outperformed its benchmark in each of the last five years.

We also specialize in understanding credit stories and identifying the best relative values in the financial services corporate bond market. This expertise allows us to provide the highest quality service to institutional investors and issuers, both investment grade and noninvestment grade.

KBW does not try to be all things to all people. We focus on a particular segment of the market. Our equity sales and trading group is particularly adept at this. The salesforce focuses solely on the financial services sector and uniquely guides clients using the perspective gained by KBW's intense research effort.

Many of the world's largest institutional investment firms and most of the best-known investors in the financial services sector are our clients. They value our research and use our trading desk to execute both listed orders and those on the NASDAQ. We execute client orders on the New York Stock Exchange (NYSE) and on all of the regional exchanges. We are market makers in over 350 NASDAQ financial services stocks and are one of the top three market makers in many of those stocks. Our NASDAQ desk often trades more financial stocks than many of the larger firms. KBW plays a significant role in a number of markets. In February 2002, we started providing market-making services in an additional 100 stocks. In addition, we put our own money to work for our clients. Our trading desk often has one of the largest overnight positions—that is, the firm is long the stock after the close—among

Wall Street's brokers and dealers in the financial stocks that we follow.

Our sales group is and was headed up by Tom Michaud. Prior to 9/11, Tom was an executive vice president and a member of KBW's board of directors. Since 9/11, he has been promoted to chief operating officer and vice chairman of the company. Normally, Tom is at his desk long before 9 A.M., leading the morning meeting. However, this was not the case on that fateful Tuesday in September 2001. Tom's enthusiasm for Michael Jackson saved his life. He had attended a Michael Jackson concert the night before. There were probably very few other executive vice presidents and directors of equity sales at that concert on September 10, but luckily for us Tom was there. After arriving home late that evening, he got a late start the next morning, arriving at the office at 8:40—a solid hour and a half after his normal arrival time. He owes his four-year-old son gratitude for surprising him in the shower that morning, causing him to miss his train. This put him on the sidewalk outside the World Trade Center rather than at his desk when the plane hit.

At the time the morning meeting is in full swing, I begin my drive to the office, generally arriving around nine. I joined the company in 1978 as an analyst on our Bank Watch service. After running that department, I moved over to our corporate finance department, eventually heading that group, which advises banks and thrifts on mergers and helps them raise capital. In 1999, along with Joe Berry, I was named co-CEO and president of the firm.

I rarely throw away old memos, articles, or any other paper document that comes my way, so my office is filled with paper (much to the dismay of some of my peers). My associates love telling how, after the World Trade Center bombing in 1993, one of the rescue workers came through the building and after viewing my office, asked if that was where the bomb went off.

Like many in our corporate finance department, Andy Senchak, our recently appointed president, has no typical workday. After driving from his home in New Jersey and taking the water taxi across the Hudson from Liberty Harbor, he would arrive in his office on the 88th floor sometime between 7:30 and 9:30 in the morning. Andy says that he manages by wandering [around the office], and his days vary according to the transactions KBW is working on or particular events at the firm.

Andy joined KBW in 1985 after leaving Rutgers University where he taught economics. Andy explained his thinking on making the move from Rutgers to KBW: "Basically, I packed up my office which was the size of a closet at Rutgers University on a Sunday night and drove with enormously high spirits down the Jersey Turnpike. I went to work at KBW the next morning, a Monday morning in January. At the same time, I realized that I'd turned from two other opportunities—one a postdoctoral fellowship at Harvard Business School and another a job as an economist at Sanford Bernstein, but I was so happy to be at Keefe I'd forgotten about those other two offers." Andy sheepishly admits that he never even thought to tell the other firm and Harvard of his choice. Andy never regretted his decision.

Andy had an office on the 88th floor, as did Michael O'Brien, another survivor, who was the president of KBW Asset Management on 9/11 and has since been promoted to CEO of our asset management subsidiary. Michael, who joined the firm around the same time as Andy, was the only member of our board of directors who was in the building at the time of the attack who managed to escape. Most of our investment bankers have schedules similar to Michael's and Andy's—much depends on the deals they are working on. Even if they manage to leave the office at a respectable hour, many spend their evenings reading analysts' reports and other material related to the financial services industries they follow.

Our investment bankers tend to come in later than the trading staff but they also stay later. Our investment banking practice is based on long-term relationships developed by a core group of managing directors. As in other areas in the firm, turnover of employees is very low. Most of our investment bankers have been with us for more than 10 years.

Our investment banking practice is focused broadly on the financial services industry. For us that means many different businesses—all of which are in the "financial" space. We do a lot of work for banks and thrifts, but we are also very active working with insurance companies, broker/dealers, asset management firms, mortgage companies, leasing companies, and a variety of commercial and consumer credit businesses.

In an advisory capacity, we counsel clients on their strategic options and related transactions. This includes a variety of services such as merger and acquisitions advice, takeover defenses, valuations, fairness opinions, corporate restructuring, and investor relations. In this capacity, we have maintained a leading role with our banking industry clients. The banking industry has consolidated at a rapid pace in the past 10 years. Since 1997, we have acted as financial advisor in 178 mergers and acquisitions of banks and thrifts. These transactions had a total deal value of over $37 billion. During this period, we have also completed 23 advisory assignments for nonbank financial institutions valued at $1.6 billion.

Mergers and acquisitions (M&A) in the bank arena are our bread and butter. Thompson Financial/First Call publishes benchmark "league tables" ranking firms by the dollar value of their annual deal activity in bank M&A. In 2001, despite the challenges we faced as a firm, we ranked fifth, up from our ranking in 2000, where we were ninth. Our 2001 accomplishments put us ahead of a number of bigger firms, such as J.P. Morgan Chase, Morgan Stanley, and Salomon, Smith Barney. In terms of sheer number of deals, we were ranked #1 in 2001. The 37 deals we advised on had a total deal value of over $6 billion. This put us well ahead of the #2 firm which had completed 16 transactions. In 2000, we placed ninth on the list, completing 19 deals valued at over $3 billion. Our 2001 results are especially noteworthy when you consider the fact that overall, it was not a banner year for deal flow in the investment banking industry. Moreover, we did remarkably well in that we closed nine of those deals after September 11 and we have already announced 12 transactions in 2002 (an even "slower" year for the industry).

The American Banker also ranks participants in the financial markets each year. Based on their analysis, we ranked first among leading financial advisors based on number of transactions in 1996, 1997, 1999, and 2001. In 1998 and 2000, we ranked second. Overall, I believe these accomplishments underscore the fact that for a relatively small firm, KBW's mergers and acquisitions practice has stacked up quite nicely against the bigger Wall Street firms.

The other part of our corporate finance effort involves the managing, placement, and sales of both public and private market financing activity for our financial institution clients. We manage offerings of a variety of capital markets products, including both underwritten public transactions as well as private placements of common stock, preferred stock, and fixed income securities. Our reputation for excellence in research carries into this arena. It enables us to build strong relationships with scores of investors seeking access to the capital markets, as well as the institutional investors who seek value in this sector.

One of our more significant accomplishments in the capital markets involves the pioneering work we have done in helping smaller community banks and thrifts access the market for a specific capital product—trust preferred stock—which, heretofore, has been available predominately to larger banking companies. Through our work with the rating agencies and investors, we have been able to place over $3 billion of this product since the summer of 2000. Since September 11 alone, we have placed $2 billion, making KBW the market leader for this innovative product. It's this type of industry knowledge and creativity that gains us the respect of both issuing companies and the institutional investors we service.

In the equity markets, we maintain a leading position as market maker. This has been an important factor in helping us obtain capital raising assignments. Since 1997, we managed or co-managed over $20 billion in offerings for our clients.

Our corporate finance group has also played a role in one of the hottest areas for thrifts and insurance companies—the process of converting from mutual ownership (e.g., where the depositors or policy holders effectively own the company) to stock ownership—whereby public investors now own shares in the company. We started a group that focused on this in the late 1980s and it grew rapidly when in 1996 we acquired Charles Webb & Company, a firm that specialized in that market. We've completed over 125 conversions and actually led the investment banking community in 1999 in the number of completed conversions as well as the amount of gross proceeds raised.

Our affiliate, KBW Asset Management, is a registered investment advisor offering investment management services to institutions and high net-worth individuals. We use a research-intensive approach to investing and have had a long history of successful investment in the financial services sector. Our success in this area is based on intimate knowledge of specific management teams, their business practices, and their franchise values. This group also serves as portfolio manager for several privately managed accounts in excess of $10 million each and offers two private limited partnerships, a general financial services fund, and a small-cap financial services fund.

The 2001 numbers for the firm were strong with revenues of more than $150 million, up $25 million from the prior year. Going into September, with sales and trading rolling and our investment banking team setting an all-time KBW record for number of deals, we really had the company well positioned.

On the lighter side, we are known for our lunches. We bring in lunch for all of our employees, not just the traders, as is the custom at some other Wall Street firms. Most of the time, our caterer supplies the meals. However, Fridays are a little different. We bring in food from all the fast-food restaurants in the area. Although we went back to our lunchtime catering almost immediately after September 11, it was a while before we reinstated "Junk Food Friday." Resuming this tradition, became a statement about our firm's desire and readiness to rebuild after our losses on September 11.

Chapter 2 reflects the thoughts and perspectives of Gene Bruyette, one of KBW's founding partners, on the creation and emergence of his firm as a premier boutique investment bank and on the future of the firm after September 11. The remaining chapters in Part I tell the story of those individuals who survived the violence that day and how they have gone on to help KBW rebuild.

FOUNDING FATHER:
A HISTORY OF KBW

Very little has been written about KBW in the main-stream press. Therefore, because Gene Bruyette is both a founding partner and a great storyteller, I asked him to provide a brief company history. Through recent and old press clippings, letters and notes unearthed from the Bruyette attic, Gene has woven a tale of the evolution of a unique corporate culture.

GENE'S STORY

I first met Harry Keefe in late 1951 at the Insurance City Open Golf Tournament, the precursor to the Greater Hartford Open. The week before, I had quit my job as a Parke Davis detail man. For the next seven days, I spent 10 to 12 hours a day as a volunteer erecting snow fences and doing whatever other work was needed at the golf course. Harry noticed me and, at the end of the tournament, came up and said, "Be in my office tomorrow at 9 o'clock."

When I asked why, in typical Keefe fashion he said, "Anybody who will work as hard as you have for nothing, I want to talk to."

When we met on Monday he said, "I need a bond salesman."

I replied, "What's a bond?" Whatever they were, they certainly hadn't taught me about them at pharmacy school.

Harry said, "You start in Boston next Monday at $50.00 a week. They'll teach you what you need to know up there."

So they did. In 1952, I joined Harry at R.L. Day, later to merge with Tucker Anthony. Harry had been with R.L. Day since 1946 where he met Norbert (Nobby) Woods, who was already working there as a corporate bond trader. Nobby had joined the company 10 years earlier, fresh out of high school. In 1949, when a client inquired about bank stock, Harry had already started to be interested in them. Although Harry didn't specialize in bank stocks, he thought he should be able to find an answer for the client relatively easily. He was wrong.

For all practical purposes, there wasn't any sophistication in bank stock analysis at that time. For decades, bank stocks have been yield vehicles. You bought them for their dividend security and not for any growth. Growth in the banking industry was limited to the ability of a bank to grow its demand and savings deposits. It was not legal under Regulation Q to bid for deposits. Consequently, growth was totally denominated by the environment in which the bank existed. In 1952, a bank in Arizona could grow faster than a bank in New York City.

Therefore, the institutional participation in bank stocks was similar to that of the bond buyers. Institutions would buy bank stocks strictly for their yield. The change in Regulation Q, which allowed banks to bid for money, made a big change in attitude toward bank stocks. In addition, it came at a time when there was practically no research. For example, First of Chicago—and I remember this vividly from Harry's talks—published about a three- or four-line balance sheet and no income account. That was the degree of information that was disseminated to shareholders. Harry also described going to Bank America in the early days and occasionally getting to see someone as high up as an assistant treasurer for 30 minutes—if he was lucky.

Harry could get an income account at First Chicago but he had to actually go there and copy off notes by hand. To obtain an historic track record, he and Sally Stowe, another one of our founders, spent untold hours in the business library in Hartford studying annual reports, Moody's presentations, Standard and Poor's presentations, and the like. I believe Harry was the first person to compute a price-earnings ratio on bank stocks.

Remember, there were no computers in those days. Sally would draw two- by three-foot charts by hand in India ink. Harry was famous for his slide rule. He never went anywhere without one. That's how primitive our research tools were in the beginning. However, slowly and surely, the demand for better information on banks was building within the institutional fraternity. There were very few sources to meet this need. Consequently, it quickly became apparent to Harry that bank research could be a growth area, one without much competition at all.

Sometime in 1959, R.L. Day had merged with Tucker Anthony—a broker firm, not dealers. They took no positions in any securities. However, Harry felt strongly that if a firm were to have integrity with investments and its recommendations, we must buy the bank stocks that we recommend and be at the same kind of risk as our customers. Thus, Harry was at odds on this issue with the firm. Eventually, that led to his leaving to establish his own firm.

Harry also had some unique ideas about how to treat people. Unlike a partnership where partners are the privileged few, shareholding in KBW was expected of employees. Part of the philosophical approach at KBW is that the *employees* are expected to risk money, especially the analysts. If you are working for KBW and are recommending to the principals that they go long on a given stock, we expect some of your money to go along for the ride.

We officially founded KBW on July 11, 1962, with a staff of eight—three partners, Harry, Nobby, and me; our corporate secretary, Sally Stowe; and four other employees—John Hawke, Allan Casey, Claire Wilcox, and Charlie Lott. The $50,000 in capital that we started with may not sound like much money today, but in 1962, it was quite a bit. Harry and I were lucky. We had invested some money in Security Insurance Company of New Haven and it turned out to be a winner. That's where the two of us got our capital contributions. Nobby had not invested with us and therefore did not have funds to purchase founder's shares—until Sally intervened. She persuaded her father to lend him the funds he needed. Nobby never forgot. Here's a little of what Harry said about him in his 1972 eulogy.

[Nobby always said] "I know what it's like not to have money. If the firm prospers, we must share with our employees." Just last week, at his suggestion, we gave an across-the-board salary increase to every employee earning less than $10,000. In trading, Nobby was an astute and vicious competitor—in life, he was a soft touch.

Nobby would be thrilled if he could see what the company has become today—the way so many people who have worked at KBW have left as millionaires.

Since Harry has been a very just and generous man all of his life, the rewards for hard work at KBW have been high and democratically distributed. The more dilution the founders took, the more they prospered. The collegiality of the organization, the manner in which it was structured, the absence of commissioned salesmen, and everybody "feeding from the same pot" created an environment far from the Wall Street norm. It also bred tremendous loyalty. After 9/11, we received a letter from a former employee, Sheila Reilly. She worked for us for three years and now lives in Alaska. Her words validate the founding ideals of the partners of KBW:

> Dear KBW family,
>
> I have never worked for a company as supportive, energized, and as intellectually stimulating as KB&W. This firm has developed a cohesive workplace where everyone is focused, productive, and successful while fostering an atmosphere where it is truly a pleasure to come to work every day. While we know our banks often give lip service to their greatest asset, KB&W truly lives it by nurturing its people and helping them to develop toward their greatest potential.

We started out with two offices, one in New York and the other in Hartford. Nobby, Harry, Sally, Allan Casey, Charlie Lott, and John Hawke were based in New York, and Claire Wilcox and I were in Hartford. Our roles were clearly divided with Harry primarily responsible for research and operations, Nobby handled trading and I managed sales.

We are often asked, why Hartford? With all the insurance companies based in Hartford, the city had more countrywide transportation options than New York. I could leave Hartford between five and six in the evening for any major city in the United States, get there that night, conduct business for a full day, and still arrive home the following evening. Planes were designed for businessmen then and it worked very well. Thus, I was home early enough to spend time with my four children who, at the firm's inception when they were all under six years of age, had called a meeting and presented their own compelling argument for me not to go to New York.

Hiring—at least in Hartford—in the early days was pretty simple. The last guy hired was responsible for lining up the next hire. Usually, a prospect would have been brought in to meet the rest of the crew before he was presented to me with a recommendation that we hire. By the time I got involved, it was almost a "done deal." The most recent hire would have to shepherd the new man into productivity. I like to call the process, "implanting the KBW DNA."

We've grown too big now to handle hiring in this manner—but we do abide by the underlying principle. We want to bring in people who will fit. This doesn't mean they have to be exactly like us; in fact, we welcome diversity, but it does mean that we want people who like each other and get along. So peer interviewing is a serious part of our hiring process.

Luckily, the securities world doesn't like monopolies. When we started out, we were welcomed into the business with open arms, both by the banks we would cover and our competition. Outside of the New York/New England area, nobody had ever really heard of us, and the competition that we had for the product was very limited. At that time, M. A. Shapiro was the primary bank advocate before the creation of KBW.

I can remember Harry telling how, our first day, a man by the name of Brad Lake, the chief financial officer of Seattle First

National Bank, a huge man, full of bluster, came walking into the office. Without ever sitting down, he barked, "Keefe, how much is the rent?"

Harry told him.

"I got it for this year," Lake said.

This was the kind of welcome we received. I recall going to see Stein Rowe in Chicago. The head trader, Tony DePresio, had never seen anybody from KBW but after speaking with Nobby and me, he said, "Until I see that you are fully established, we will be a client."

Like many of the other traders, including the Putnam Fund's Frank Mullen, Eaton and Howard's Dick Richards and Malcomb Robinson from Fidelity Funds, DePresio wanted an alternative source for trading purposes. Business was strong. Our clients were very good to us. For the first five to seven years, they adopted us. After that, we had to make it in our own.

Traveling with Nobby was a treat. He was color blind, so his wife would pack for him in a unique manner. To assist him in matching his clothes correctly, she would attach a paper cut with crimping shears to each piece. The papers were cut like a jigsaw puzzle so that he could match his clothes. Watching him unpack that suitcase was quite an experience

We started making a market in bank stocks on day one. Very quickly, we caught the eye of a bastion of the financial world, M. A. Shapiro. He was a very smart man with a lot of capital. Although we had very little capital, he knew that we were going to be able to generate business. However, he also realized that we would be unable to execute everything we generated and that he could be the primary beneficiary.

The afternoon of the tenth of July, he called Harry and said, "At the close today, I'll give you any positions you want to start with on the bid side of the market when it closes."

Thus, we were able to establish our inventory and at a good price, too. Shapiro's largesse didn't end there. We were just babes in the woods in terms of how to clear a transaction and how to handle other back office duties. Shapiro had a back office wizard who worked for him and he invited Sally Stowe to visit his shop and learn. Inside she saw every detail of every transaction: who they were with, how many shares, how to keep proper records, how to check on the clearing agent, and finally, how to clear our own transactions.

Shapiro knew Harry very well. For one thing, our first office in Chase Manhattan was on the same floor as his at the other end of the same hall. It was easy for him to watch us as we slowly, and then not so slowly, began to grow.

Our specialty was regional bank stocks, an area that few analysts covered. I'd go visit a city and the first thing I would do after landing at the airport was to find a cabbie who thoroughly knew the area. We'd drive around the city and I'd become oriented with the local color. That way I would be a little better prepared for my first meeting. Such small details reaped large rewards in this business.

When the company was first formed, there were fixed commissions on the New York Stock Exchange. KBW dealt on the "third market." The third market was when you dealt in listed stocks over the counter, and all of this was before the NASDAQ market was started in 1971.

The fixed commission rates were changed at various dollars but the majority were fifty cents. A $25 stock would carry a fifty-cent commission and a $50 stock might have a seventy-five-cent commission and so on. Back then, the specialist would quote a stock twenty-five to twenty-five and a half. Then the broker would come in, buy it at twenty-five and a half and charge a fifty-cent commission. What KBW would do is make a market at twenty-five to twenty-five and a half with no commission. Sometimes we'd expand the market just a little bit, and quote twenty-five to twenty-five and three-quarters. Therefore, the investor would save half a commission. Thus, there was an advantage to dealing with the over the counter person as opposed to going to the big board. This was a good business for us.

Harry was very vocal and the first to say how ridiculous the stock exchange was—until, of course, we joined. In his defense, by the time we joined, fixed commissions had been thrown away. Our first membership was on the Pacific Stock Exchange, followed by the exchange in Philadelphia, and finally New York. Both KBW and Shapiro were forces in the third market in the banking industry.

We were always innovators. We began publishing our financial statements in 1970, allowing Harry to brag that we were one of the first broker-dealers to do so.

Joe Berry Sr. joined the firm in 1972, after a circuitous route. He'd grown up very simply in Woodside, Queens. His father had died when he was nine years old and he did not have a lot of guidance. He went to Archbishop Molloy High School, which he credits for turning him around although he continued to be an average student in high school. After graduation, he started taking a few courses at Queens College but wasn't really focused on school.

He also started working at a men's dress shirt store called Plushers. He was known for being well dressed even then. He noticed men from Wall Street spending a lot on shirts at the shop. This was at a time when he was being paid an hourly wage as a clerk, although the owner was taking him along on buying meetings because of his style.

These young Wall Street men with money to spend made an impression on Joe. They made him reconsider what he was doing and gave him the incentive to return to Queens College and get a degree in math. He began teaching at Christ the King High School during the day and putting himself through St. John's for an MBA. He wanted to work on Wall Street. After he got his degree, he sent out 60 to 70 resumes. He got only one response. Harry, upon seeing his resume, remarked, "You know, we've never hired a math teacher. Let's bring him in."

In 1972, Joe Berry Sr. started in equity sales, and the rest, as they say, is history. Joe began working as the personal assistant to Charlie Lott, one of the eight original KBW employees. He started out making calls for Charlie. "Just get me in the door," is what Charlie told him. Joe dug up the leads. Once Joe had lined up a call, Charlie would go and make his sales pitch, often with Joe accompanying him. After four or five years of listening to Charlie give his spiel, he knew it so well, the two men became partners. Joe had learned a lot.

Both men were aggressive and loved competing against each other, in everything. On long trips, they would play gin rummy. Charlie says he was the better player but Joe always had an excuse: he was tired, he'd had a drink and Charlie didn't drink, or some other reason. One day, on a trip back from seeing a client, there was trouble and the two men spent eight hours on a plane. Charlie, just as determined as Joe, decided he was going to prove once and for all who was the better gin rummy player. He matched Joe drink for drink for the whole eight hours. This was some feat for a man who generally does not imbibe. Today, he says he does not remember who won that game; he also does not know how he got home in one piece. He does remember that it was one of his toughest drives ever.

Charlie says the two spent so much time together that they were like husband and wife, often arguing but never going home mad. He calls Joe a "once-in-a-lifetime" friend. He would often tease Joe about his Queens accent. When Charlie decided to step down as chairman of the firm in 1998, Jim McDermott became chairman and Joe took over the president's position.

Years later, Joe Sr. would pass on to his own son, a new hire at KBW, the lesson he learned from his hard climb: "Even if you have nothing and no direction, if you put your mind to something, you can really get there."

The years 1972 and 1973 were very tough in the securities business. We did virtually no hiring during that time but we didn't lay anybody off either. After that period,, the business really started to expand, with the creation of our Bank Watch service. We eventually added some 30 additional employees.

Harry used to go each May to London for a big symposium that we would sponsor. We would bring over American bankers and it was a big deal. Dozens of institutional investors would come and listen to our speakers. Periodically, he would also go to address a group of bankers in Switzerland. He was very good at it. In 1972, he asked me to go in his place. Speaking to a group of international bankers was not exactly my forte but I had listened to Harry enough that I could prepare a speech. Harry thought it was time I did this, so off I went. The speech was set for a Monday morning.

While the world slept the night before my talk, President Nixon devalued the dollar. Remember I'm a pharmacist by training. I'd never taken an economics course, much less one in accounting. I picked up a newspaper before going to give my talk and the headlines screamed, "NIXON DEVALUES THE DOLLAR." Because of the time differences, I couldn't reach anyone in the office.

What was I to do? I did the only thing I could think of—I gave my speech as written, which, of course, made no reference to the devaluation that had just occurred. Afterwards, I could only hope for the best. The question-and-answer period that followed was not pretty. The Swiss, unfortunately, read the newspapers. The first question was "What is the impact, Mr. Bruyette, of the American devaluation of the dollar on the American banking industry?"

I tried to hide behind the podium. When that didn't work, I wanted to disappear. When the meeting finally ended, I got Harry on the telephone and told him what had transpired. All I could hear from across the ocean was gales of laughter. Needless to say, I never was invited to speak in Switzerland again.

When we started, KBW's trading room was nothing like the one the firm has today. Back then, all trades between firms were done verbally. Today, verbal contact between the traders of two firms is less frequent. Everything is done on a computer. The early KBW process was nothing like that.

Nobby Woods and John Hawke were KBW's trading team, Nobby was a very gregarious, emotional kind of guy. John Hawke was his voice, because if Nobby got on the telephone with another trader, his voice would give him away, unable to conceal either his enthusiasm or lack of it regarding the trade.

He'd have been a lousy poker player. Everybody would know when he had a good hand. However, John Hawke was the stoic type. In extreme emotion, John's voice might go up one decibel. They made a great team, one as the decision maker, and the other as the voice. Nobby was regarded as the trading dean. Again, I turn to Harry's 1972 eulogy. Here's what he had to say about Nobby's gift for trading:

Since the founding of the firm in 1962, Nobby has had the responsibility of managing our trading account where we always had a position at least equal to the full amount of the firm's capital. We have never had a losing quarter, have always made money in down markets, and this year saw our profits rise to a record level—70 percent over 1971. Few traders on Wall Street could match that record. From his humble start as a high school graduate, he had reached the top in one of the most demanding, competitive, and precarious careers.

The investment community will remember Nobby for his trading skill—we'll remember him as the driving force that kept us going. He hated to miss a trade. Bruyette called him "The Whip." His very intensity of purpose was the cause of his physical downfall. You could no more get Nobby Woods to take it easy than make a thoroughbred racehorse walk. When the market was open, it was impossible to divert his attention from his beloved numbers. He hated to go to lunch for fear he would miss something.

The firm suffered its first major blow in December 1972. Nobby had a fatal heart attack while eating in a restaurant. In one moment, he was gone. It was extremely traumatic. He was such a beautiful man.

As we became better known all over the United States in the mid-seventies, we opened an office in London. We decided to start a JV with another firm who specialized in insurance stocks—Conning and Company—a company with roots in Hartford, Connecticut, as well. It had a correspondent in London. The company did essentially the same kind of thing as we did but in insurance stocks. The only difference was that Conning was not a dealer, just a broker. The company wanted to represent our research in that market, and we worked out an arrangement with them to do

so. After a period, it was decided that we should have a home presence in London located in their physical facilities. We would market our research over there. It worked well, for a while.

Eventually, the relationship became strained. Conning
wanted increasingly more. As the banking industry got more
complex, it became harder for us to be well represented abroad.
Conning used the same people to represent their insurance and
to do our bank research. We finally decided to send our own
people over. Some time after that, our people in the London office heard that Conning was entertaining a merger. If Conning
merged with a British brokerage firm, where would that have left
us? The contemplation of a merger was not mentioned to us and
that did not sit well with us, and our business relationship was
severed.

The next impetus for growth came with the change in Regulation Q, which brought certificates of deposit into being, effectively allowing banks to bid for funds. Some call Franklin National
Bank on Long Island, a pioneer in the field, the father of CDs.

However, there came a time when banks were in trouble. This
was when the Federal Deposit and Insurance Corporation (FDIC)
came to Harry and literally funded us for what wound up becoming our Bank Watch Service: the bank credit analysis and credit
rating service. The FDIC was concerned about its in-house capacity to make necessary judgments regarding banks. It wanted
someone who had the street smarts to be able to address this matter. Apparently it had tried to hire groups like J.P. Morgan, but
was turned down. J.P. Morgan declined because it would be faced
with having to credit rate its own correspondents and didn't want
a real conflict of interest. So an independent partner was needed.

We put Michael Conner, one of our investment bankers, in
charge of the project. As things progressed, it became much too

large for Mike to oversee alone. So in 1978 we brought John Duffy in from Standard & Poors. When John moved on to our corporate finance group, Greg Root took over the Bank Watch division.

We carried the concept further than was originally conceived by the FDIC, turning it into a rating service similar to Moody's. We used an A through D scale and a bank could not afford to have its Bank Watch rating go below a C. Such a decline could effectively cut it off from funding. Therefore, ratings became a very serious business. They could mean life or death for banking companies.

I remember one example of this vividly. Harry was recovering from open-heart surgery in 1984 so I was elected to go to Continental Illinois to hear their final plea for a better rating. John was there along with Greg Root. The bankers pleaded for reconsideration of what we had forewarned them we were going to do, but we had no choice. Given our analysis, we were forced to lower its rating; the bank soon disappeared.

One of the most dramatic events we were involved with was the case of Texas Commerce. We had been their investment banker from the time they were a two hundred million dollar bank. The bank had gotten into all kinds of trouble with subpar lending and commercial real estate. Harry and I visited and told them we were seriously considering taking them down to a D rating. The final decision was to be made the following Wednesday. That morning Ben Love, the company chairman, called to find out whether in fact we did intend to make them a D. I said yes.

He said, "Gene, I wish I never met you."

It was devastating, but it had to be done. Our integrity was at stake. Shortly thereafter, Salomon Brothers, acting as Texas Commerce's new investment banker—the role we had played for so many years—earned seven million dollars for advising Texas

Commerce on its merger with Chemical Bank. Sometimes integrity comes at a very high price.

Those are just two examples of what our ratings could cost us. We were even threatened with lawsuits by banks that thought they could intimidate us into refraining from doing what we believed was right.

Probably the low point for the firm, at least before I retired, was the failure of Bank of New England in early 1991. We were the bank's investment banker and advised its executives on many of its acquisitions. Unfortunately, with the purchase of Conifer Bank in Worchester, the bank ended up assuming a huge real estate exposure that ultimately took it down.

The obvious problem of being both a credit rater and an investment banker is that the credit rater is a *critic* and the investment banker is an *advocate.* Those trains just don't meet. Some of us felt the conflict was too much. Therefore, when KBW was approached to sell Bank Watch in 1989, the KBW board of directors agreed. This was not an easy decision. It was discussed for several months before we made the final determination.

Once we'd made our decision, we reported it to the employees. It was important to our management team that the employees of Bank Watch be well treated. They cashed in their KBW stock for a handsome sum and all departing employees kept their jobs. Bank Watch departed as a cohesive group, same bosses, same employees.

We had Salomon Bothers working for us on the deal and Harry worked very hard on enhancing the first bid, which came from Standard & Poors. Finally, in March of 1989, after receiving several bids for our Bank Watch service, we sold it to Thompson Financial. We had something like a 26 percent enhancement of book value after taxes on the sale. The purchase price was not bad for a business that the FDIC nudged us into only 10 or 15 years earlier.

By this time, we had made our mark in the investment community. In 1982, we took top honors as the best Wall Street banking industry stock analysis firm in *Bank Letter*, a publication of the *Institutional Investor*. We regularly win this award and in 1984 achieved a new milestone—we won first place twice. Again we had earned the top ranking for our banking industry equity research and in the first six months of that year, we completed the most banking industry merger and acquisition transactions in the business. Our second first place award was based on a count made by *The Corporate Financing Week*, another publication of *Institutional Investor*, of tombstones placed in the *Wall Street Journal*. Clearly, we were a force to be reckoned with.

At that point, our corporate finance department consisted of 10 professionals and dealt exclusively with commercial banking and banking related mergers and acquisitions, financial advisory work, and financing. In the early eighties, we started an informal training program in Hartford. It produced some of our best hires including, Joe Lenihan, who we lost on 9/11, Michael O'Brien, our current asset management CEO, and Phil Cuthbertson, one of the retirees who came back to help us after 9/11.

Today our Hartford office has 15 employees. In 1984, we had 13 equity analysts following 175 banking companies. Today, we have 34 analysts following 350 companies.

One of the innovations that I was responsible for was the "Bruyette dinners." Most securities firms invite their clients to a dinner and then have somebody from the company make a pitch of some kind. My idea was to turn this concept around. We would ask them questions such as what they currently considered the best bank stock buys, or where they thought interest rates were going. We'd let them talk things out among themselves. In many cities, the fraternity of bank investors rarely meet to put their heads together in such a manner. Our dinners were a first. KBW still hosts these dinners in 20 cities around the country and in the United Kingdom.

Another tradition of KBW is the annual stock-picking contest. Each January, the firm asks its employees to pick the best and worst performing financial stocks for the next 12 months. One of the firm's finest moments came when the first overall winner was announced in 1988. Fran Haros, who died on 9/11, the firm's receptionist, won the first overall prize. We were all happy for Fran, but there were some mightily bruised egos in the shop that day.

In 1989, Harry left KBW to form an investment firm, Keefe Managers, which now runs a $150 million hedge fund specializing in financial services stocks. That year we lost another of our cornerstones, Sally Stowe, who retired after marrying Robert J. Clemence. As noted, Sally was a founder of KBW and went on to become a director, an executive vice president, and our CFO. What a remarkable woman! Although self-taught, she advanced in a man's world long before working women were readily accepted. After graduating from Edgewood Park Junior College, she worked her way up after starting at a Hartford bank as a secretary.

Her next position was as a registered representative and analyst of bank stocks and municipal bonds at KBW. Although she started in Hartford, she quickly moved to the New York office. As her responsibilities grew, she became our expert in a variety of areas including corporate and personal taxes, life insurance, health insurance, and employee benefit plans. She was one of the first women to become a director of a New York Stock Exchange member firm.

Sally was an extremely compassionate person. She not only persuaded her father to lend Nobby the money to buy his founding shares in 1962, she also showed her kindness when we hired

Phil Cuthbertson in 1980. Phil was fresh out of graduate school and broke. He had an old car and a mountain of student loans. He came for his interview in his one and only suit. Toward the end of the meeting, he asked about the dress code. I told him it was what he was wearing.

I remember him saying that he would not be able to take the job because he could not afford to buy new clothes. He says he asked me for $1,000. I agreed to give him the money. When I told Sally, she immediately sent a check for $2,000. Upon receiving the check, Phil called up to inquire about the discrepancy. Sally had decided that after taxes, $1,000 wouldn't be adequate and had raised the stipend to an amount she thought appropriate. Phil told us later that when he related this story to his mother, she cried.

Sally exemplified what was best about our corporate culture. She was often instrumental in the firm doing wonderful things for its employees. For example, we had a fellow working in our mail-room who had an interesting family pedigree. He joined us in 1979 describing himself as an itinerant photographer. His father was a friend to Bob Hope and was being honored at a special ceremony, I believe in Phoenix. Like most mailroom positions, ours didn't pay that much and he didn't have the funds to buy a ticket to go to see his father get the award. Sally got wind of the situation, purchased a plane ticket, and gave it to him along with a little cash. Although this fellow didn't get exceedingly rich while working for us, his pension and profit sharing have given him financial freedom. He's 57 and still occasionally writes to Sally.

As our company grew, so did our offices. We made a series of moves before ending up in the World Trade Center in the mid-1980s, after occupying space in the Marine Midland building, the old U.S. Steel building at 91 Liberty Street, and finally into Tower 2, first on the 85th and then on the 88th and 89th floors.

I retired in 1991. It was time. When Harry left, I had become chairman. I tried to work from Hartford, but with offices in San Francisco, London, and New York, I was never home. We had no social life. I was so exhausted, that I got sick. I'd been a three to four pack-a-day smoker for 40 years and got bronchitis that turned into bronchial spasms. After I got out of the hospital, I took a few weeks off and went to Florida. A doctor friend of mine said, "Why don't you retire? Do you need work financially? Do you need work psychologically?"

I said, "I don't think so."

He persisted. "Well then, tell me why don't you stop?"

I had no answer. So, I went out, hit some golf balls, and thought things over. Then I went home and said to my wife, Kathleen, "I'm going to retire."

She said, "Are you sure?"

When I said yes, she said, "Well that's fine."

And that was it.

On the day of the World Trade Center bombing in 1993, we were located on the 85th floor of the South Tower. Although our employees had some harrowing experiences, like Bob Planer and Joe Berry Sr. being stuck in an elevator for many hours, and Michael O'Brien waiting five hours to be rescued, our group escaped intact. KBW took advantage of Wachtell's largesse in offering us temporary space in midtown Manhattan. Our sales and trading group was temporarily located in Pershing's offices in New Jersey. At the time, it seemed like the worst thing that could have happened to our firm. Little did we know what lay ahead.

By 1998, KBW had grown to the point where we thought we could go public. Therefore, we started making plans as did other brokerage firms. However, the market turned against us and we decided to wait for more favorable conditions.

The following spring, the market looked better for KBW. We were only days from pricing our second attempt at an IPO, in May 1999, when the then CEO, James J. McDermott, revealed to the KBW board of directors that the Securities and Exchange Commission (SEC) was investigating a friend of his. This is devastating news for any company but especially for one that prides itself on its integrity as we do. The revelation forced us to pull the IPO from the market. Jim left the company two months later intending to take a position with Allen & Co. As part of his severance agreement, we agreed not to talk publicly about the investigation. We did not know the full extent of the problem at that point.

We did not give a reason for pulling the IPO. What could we say that would not damage the reputation of the firm? This led to wild speculation in the press that perhaps there was a better deal in the offing. However, the truth was revealed when Jim was arrested that December. He was charged with seven counts of securities fraud for providing insider-trading information to a reputed pornographic film star. Some wondered if we would ever live this down. A few employees left the firm. Al DiAntonio left us in January 2000. I am relieved and proud to say that the McDermott incident was an isolated event and not one other employee was ever implicated in the mess.

The incident cost Jim dearly. The IPO was planned at $85 million. As the fourth largest shareholder, he would have netted $16 million. Instead, he went to jail. He was sentenced to eight months in prison and was released in 2001 after serving five months.

When Jim left the firm, Joe Berry Sr. became chairman of the board and co-CEO with John Duffy, who also assumed the position of president.

Our people moved into our two new floors in the World Trade Center in March 2000. It seemed like a new beginning. We had put our past behind us and were showing the world and the financial community that we were still a force to be reckoned with. Our clients stuck with us. We continued to win awards. We were still a major player in our marketplace.

The board began talking to Banque National de Paris (BNP)/Paribas about a potential merger. But after 9/11, there were doubts on both sides and the merger was called off.

Harry and I were devastated by the events of 9/11. We had hired many of the people who perished. Harry, Sally, and I returned to KBW together on October 10, 2001. We offered our support and reminded the firm of all the difficulties and challenges we face when founding KBW. We held a firmwide conference call with the employees, the people charged with rebuilding KBW. Here is part of what we told them:

Harry and I greatly appreciate this opportunity to personally tell each and every member of the KBW family how enormously proud we are of you.

In the face of unthinkable events, you have, through your words and deeds, proudly celebrated the memory of your departed friends. In the process, you have also done yourselves proud.

I confidently use the phrase "KBW family" for if there ever was any doubt that the people of KBW were family you have put that doubt forever to rest.

In the last weeks, we have been witness to your many selfless sacrifices, your outpouring of loving support to victims' families, your wonderful Shepherds program, uplifting, inspirational eulogies, and much more. Your love, hugs, and tears have shown the world that you are indeed a great family.

It was very, very gratifying to see the turnout of so many KBW alumni. A number of them, as you know, have gone on to achieve notable positions on Wall Street. However, it is clear that those who have spent even modest periods in their careers as KBW employees have become bonded irrevocably to the wonderful people of this company.

Our pride in your accomplishments has grown with each passing year. Harry, Sally, and I left this company about a decade ago when perhaps it could have been compared to a flower in bud. In the ensuing years, the good people of KBW brought that bud to full and brilliant bloom.

We are so proud to be a part of this family.

Harry passed away on March 8, 2002, just a month and a day before his eightieth birthday. He did however live to see how well his people had recovered and how they took care of each other and the extended KBW family. He was exceedingly proud of the way they rallied together after 9/11.

I've been wearing an American flag pin since 9/11. I spend my winters in Florida now but came back in March to attend Harry's funeral and give the eulogy. At that time, Robin Bell, a long-time employee in our Hartford office, gave me a new pin, which I wear proudly. It looks like a ribbon with the colors of the American flag and through the middle it says KBW. The pin is not just a Hartford creation, our employees in New York have them, too.

Without a doubt, the firm will survive and prosper. I am very proud to have my name appear on the front door of such a great firm.

3

WATCHING THE HORROR UNFOLD

As is my normal routine, on the morning of September 11, I headed down the Cross County Parkway going west onto the Henry Hudson Parkway and then onto the West Side Highway coming south into Manhattan.

I had attended a charity golf outing on Monday, September 10, for friends of ours, the O'Briens, who had lost a child a few years before. It was a fundraiser for a foundation they set up, dedicated to finding a cure for Cockayne Syndrome, the illness that had taken their four-and-a-half-year-old child. We had a nice day with them despite the rain that had prevented us from playing much golf.

Because we had come home late the prior evening, I was a little behind schedule on the morning of the 11th. As I was coming down the West Side Highway, just a few minutes before 9 A.M., an announcer on the radio reported that there was smoke coming from the World Trade Center or the surrounding area. The helicopter pilot giving the traffic report said that he would fly south to investigate further. Within a few minutes, there were reports on the radio that a plane had struck the Trade Center. I immediately thought that if this were true, it was probably a private plane and must involve some sort of pilot error. Since it was a perfectly clear morning, I couldn't envision the event involving a large commercial jet.

Within minutes, there were reports that it was in fact a commercial airliner that had struck the Trade Center, crashing into the upper floors of the North Tower where there now raged a substantial fire. From my position on the road, I couldn't see the Trade Center, my vision of downtown Manhattan was blocked by buildings in midtown. However, as I continued down the West Side Drive, I spotted helicopters flying to the scene.

At 59th Street, I could easily see the fire in the North Tower and decided to get off the West Side Drive, park in midtown, and find some means of getting downtown. I had already called the office from my cell phone, first dialing our Chairman, Joe Berry's number. He was on the line but one of our secretaries, Jackie Donovan, picked up the telephone. After I told her what I had heard on the radio, she reported that from our offices on the eighty-ninth floor of the South Tower they could see the damage to the North Tower and that it was a horrific scene.

Although things appeared to be relatively safe in the South Tower, I told her I would call again in a few minutes just to be sure. After exiting the West Side Highway, I parked my car on West 30th Street. In this short amount of time, I heard the radio report that a second plane had hit the South Tower—the building in which our offices were located.

My initial reaction was disbelief. How could there be two accidents like this? Within a few minutes, there were radio reports confirming there had indeed been a second disaster. I parked the car and decided to try to take the subway from midtown to the

Trade Center. On Seventh Avenue, I passed St. Francis Church and stopped in to say a quick prayer for our people in the South Tower. When I left the church, I tried futilely to get on the subway at Seventh Avenue, near Penn Station.

At that point, I walked to Sixth Avenue thinking that since trains on that line didn't go all the way down to the Trade Center there would be a better chance that I could get near the City Hall area and then walk the rest of the way. At Sixth Avenue, I boarded a train in the station. The doors remained open and after several minutes, there was an announcement saying that there had been an accident at the World Trade Center and all train service was being suspended.

I left the train station and tried called home to let my wife and my daughter Caitlin know that I was all right. Like many others that day, I failed to get a signal on my cell phone and began looking for a pay phone. Eventually, I found a pay phone at one of the hotels near Madison Square Garden. By now, it was probably close to ten o'clock. There was a television on in the lobby of the hotel picturing clouds of billowing smoke erupting from the Trade Center.

When my call home finally went through, Caitlin answered and told me that one of the Towers had collapsed. She asked me which building our offices were in. Were they in the Tower with the antenna on top or the other building? By now, I was so traumatized that frankly I couldn't remember whether our building had the antenna or not.

I asked her if she had been in touch with her brother, Christopher, who was already at work in the South Tower. She said no that they had tried to call but had been unable to get through. I too had tried unsuccessfully to call the office from my car again after my initial conversation with Jackie. Given the collapse of the building, I was sure I couldn't get near the site. I talked briefly to my wife who was terribly concerned about Christopher and I told her I would be home as soon as I could.

After hanging up the telephone, I headed out to retrieve my car. I was walking south on Seventh Avenue at approximately 30th or 31st Street when I noticed that the people in the street were looking south. You could see the Trade Center. As I hurried along, I saw the second Tower collapse. It no longer mattered whether our offices were in the building with the antenna or not. Both buildings were gone.

In complete disbelief and filled with a sense of powerlessness that I've never felt before, I returned to St. Francis Church. I went in to pray and try to collect myself realizing what had just happened and what it could mean—not only to my son, but also to many of my coworkers and thousands of others.

After leaving the church, I returned to the garage, got in my car, and headed for home. About halfway up the West Side Highway, the police closed the road leaving thousands of cars stranded. It was probably about an hour or so before they reopened the highway. I spent this time praying and trying to reach people on my cell phone.

I made it to my home in Westchester around 12:30 or one o'clock in the afternoon. I tried to console my wife and daughter and asked if they had heard from Christopher or anyone else. I then called my daughter, Kara, who was in college at the University of Rhode Island and my son, Kevin, a junior at St. Michael's College in Vermont. I told them what had happened in New York and asked that they both come home.

Meanwhile, in midtown Manhattan, our vice chairman and director of corporate finance, Andy Senchak, was trying to make some sense out of what was going on. Instinctively, even as the disaster unfolded, he was making plans for the care of our KBW family. On Monday, the day before the attack, he had gone to the office early do some work before leaving to give a deposition at the law firm of Wachtell Lipton, located in midtown Manhattan on 52nd Street.

One day wasn't adequate to finish his testimony at Wachtell, so Andy had to go back a second day. Because he wanted to get the deposition over with as early as possible, everyone agreed that they would start early on Tuesday, setting a starting time of nine o'clock rather than ten o'clock. So Andy went straight to the law offices rather than coming to the office first. He arrived at Wachtell at about 8:45.

Andy was waiting to give the deposition when his assistant Kathleen called from Hoboken, telling him that a plane had hit Tower One, the other tower. He had been trying to phone the office on another matter and was getting no answer. At the time, this had upset him, but now he knew why no one was answering the telephones. He spoke with the receptionist and the attorney with whom he was working, and they watched the events unfold on the television in the attorney's office. Ed Herlihy, the Wachtell partner who handled much of our business, was returning from a breakfast meeting when he heard the news. Knowing that Andy was in the office, he immediately went to get him. Together they watched the second plane hit Tower Two.

At this point, Andy kept communications going with the people in our Hartford office. At the same time, he was counting and calculating how long it would take people to get out of the building. After the second plane hit, he tried to figure out whether or not those employees who had left the building after the first building was struck would have had enough time to reach safety before the second plane hit. It seemed as though there was adequate time. But, had they left?

Then the reports started coming in. Andy was alone at Wachtell that morning except for another lawyer, David Murphy, whose brother Chris worked at KBW as an analyst. The two men spent the day sharing information, which as we now know was largely incorrect.

Ed told me that almost immediately, Andy became a clear-headed leader—the quarterback for our team. When Ed saw our building collapse, he turned immediately to Andy and said, "Andy, we're here for you, this is your home, we're family. Make yourself at home." Through his tears, Andy accepted.

The people at Wachtell quickly sprang into action, taking the best care they could of what remained of the KBW family. The firm cleared the conference rooms on the 33rd floor, which became a *de facto* mini crisis center for our staff.

In Andy's conversations with our people in Hartford, it was decided that we needed to get organized and attempt to find out what was going on in the World Trade Center offices.

Andy got in touch with Joe Moeller and asked him to rally some of the other associates and to go down to Ground Zero to see what they could find out.

Joe was a little taken back at this request. At the time, Andy says this course of action seemed reasonable. As we now know, people were being evacuated from the area. No one was allowed in. Eventually, Joe had to call back and tell Andy that he was not able to get anywhere near our offices. However, Andy was not giving up. He also directed Joe to check in with the hospitals.

Around this time, our Hartford office had begun to compile lists, breaking the names of KBW people into two categories: safety confirmed and unconfirmed. Andy was able to notify his parents and wife of his safety right away. His brother, who was on his way down to the Trade Center to meet him for lunch, saw the building collapse. He had a few bad hours before he learned of Andy's safety.

Andy spent the rest of the day at Wachtell coordinating our information recovery efforts. It was the second time Wachtell had offered a helping hand when KBW needed space. In 1993, they had provided us with short-term space when we were temporarily displaced after the World Trade Center bombing. Once again, we became refugees occupying their conference rooms. The staff at Wachtell also took care of Andy that day. They fed him, kept him company, and at the end of the day, found him a hotel room. He did not go home to New Jersey that night, preferring to stay close by.

Our general counsel, Mitch Kleinman made a fateful decision that morning. He decided to take the local train, instead of the express, from Grand Central Station. It ran late and consequently, Mitch came out of the train station just after the first building had been hit.

Like everyone else, Mitch stood by helplessly and watched the disaster unfold. He was able to listen to the news on his Walkman, and thinking that perhaps all tall buildings were targets, he joined the crowd walking uptown, eventually catching a bus. In New York, you need exact change to pay for your ride—something that a good number of those boarding the bus with Mitch did not have. Ever the Good Samaritan, Mitch used his Metrocard to pay for about 15 people who did not have change. He got off the bus with a long list of names and telephone numbers. The group had agreed that whoever got to a working telephone first would call the families of the other riders to let them know that they were safe.

I'm not sure that most people would have the presence of mind to do what Mitch did next. He went to a cash machine and got $1,000, then stopped at a store and bought extra clothes and a charger for his cell phone. He calls it his mini-disaster plan. He was able to take calls on his cell phone and agreed with Andy to meet the next morning at Wachtell's office—although he ultimately went to Hartford that Wednesday.

Mitch ended up on the Upper West Side at his sister-in-law's apartment. What he did next speaks volumes about the corporate culture of our firm. After leaving his sister-in-law around ten that evening, he stopped in at the home of two of our IT people, Joan Feldman and Rich Fehler, who share a townhouse. Joan lives upstairs with her husband and Rich occupies the downstairs. Although both Joan and Rich were visibly upset, their actions were amazing. Along with Mitch and our Hartford office, Joan and Rich are among the unsung heroes of our rebuilding efforts. Eventually, Mitch took his brother-in-law's car and drove home arriving a little before midnight. He says that like many other people, "he didn't bother to sleep that night." Instead, he worked out an outline of what we needed to do to rebuild our firm.

Around the city, our alumni, our clients, and a few strangers were watching what was going on and thinking about us. A sales trader on our equity desk for several years in the 1990s, Al DiAntonio had left us with great regret. He had been with the firm for just a little more than six years and had a very good experience working at KBW. He often said that he loved everyone he worked with. He was across the river when the planes struck and had an up-close view of the entire disaster. Al immediately thought of his KBW family and later explained what ultimately happened:

I saw the results of the first plane. I called the trading desk because truthfully I knew it was the tower with the antenna but couldn't remember which was ours and which wasn't. They answered the telephone, with stress in their voices but said that everything was fine, that the Port Authority had said that things were secure and they were going about their business. At that point, the market was still preparing to open. Futures were strong, I remember that clearly. It looked like a good day, unlike most of August and September. Still, I couldn't help looking across the river as I continued to make calls, when I saw the second plane veer and crash into the second building. At that point, I expected the worst for our friends.

We were in a tall building in Jersey City and were told to evacuate. There was some concern that more trouble might be coming. So we left and watched the World Trade Center from the other side of the river in the parking lot, waiting to see if we could go back to work. Eventually, we were sent home.

When I reached the house, my wife rushed out crying, screaming, and "they are all dead." The building had collapsed. My wife told me that I had to go back right away and help the firm. I didn't think that was an appropriate call for me to make at that point. But, here she was volunteering me. She had made up her mind immediately; I decided to go as soon as they asked me.

Other alumni including Phil Cuthbertson, Larry Vitale, and Joe Duwan were also watching and thinking of us and eventually came back to help.

In Boston, John Ragan watched in horror with the few employees who had joined him in officially opening our Boston office just a week earlier.

I managed to reach Andy from my home several times that afternoon to find out what he had learned about who was in the building that morning, who was safe, and who might be missing. Since the attacks had taken place around nine in the morning, all of our traders, salespersons, and research people would typically have been at their desks. In these conversations with Andy, I learned that some of our people who were safe had been contacting our offices in Hartford or Boston to let fellow employees know that they had survived and report on what was happening. We decided to use our Hartford office as an information center in terms of the status of the employees. Andy also spoke with Joe Spalluto and Jim Healey that afternoon, two of our senior people in the Hartford office. He worked with them in terms of establishing a status report on each of the employees. That became our information base.

The initial news was not good. Some of the Hartford people had been on the telephone with the trading people in the New York office when the second plane hit so we knew without a doubt that those people were in the office.

Emotionally, that day and I would say for the balance of that week, it was extremely difficult to comprehend that what was happening was real. Who could have imagined anything even close to this in terms of the scope of tragedy and number of those killed so close to home? These were people, who in some cases, I had known for more than 20 years.

Joe Berry, our Chairman and my co-CEO, joined the firm in 1972 and was there when I joined in late 1978. Besides Joe, there were dozens of people who'd been at KBW for more than 10 years—people with whom I was very close and who deeply respected. I had known them as long as I had known my own family, seeing many of them day in and day out, in the office, and on the road. It was almost impossible to imagine that these folks were no longer with us. Obviously, I was also dealing with my own emotions regarding the loss of our son, Christopher.

So many of our KBW family were affected by the tragedy: women had lost their husbands, sons and daughters had lost their fathers and mothers, parents had lost children, siblings had lost brothers and sisters, and husbands had lost their wives. Ultimately, KBW lost 67 of its family that day out of the 125 employees who were in the building that day. To think that all of these families had lost a loved one and that we would never see these people again. The grief I felt is just impossible to put in words.

The question that still haunts many is why didn't more people leave when the first Tower was hit. Why did they stay? In hindsight, they clearly should have left. However, given the facts on hand at the time, the decision to stay is understandable. Who could fathom that four commercial airliners would be successfully hijacked almost simultaneously with the express purpose of destroying the World Trade Center along with other sites?

When the first Tower was hit, virtually everyone assumed it was an isolated incident. Combine this with the knowledge that when the Trade Center was bombed in 1993, the best course of action had been to remain in the office. Those who left in 1993 had a horrifying time descending stairwells filled with smoke and debris. Also the safety system at the World Trade Center was telling our people to stay where they were because the building was secure. Even employees who were going down the stairs were encouraged to go back up.

Given these facts, the decision to remain in the building was understandable. For this reason, by the day's end, with recovery efforts underway, many of us still had some hope. We were grasping at straws.

4

INSIDE TOWER TWO

On the morning of Tuesday, September 11, our traders, salespeople, and researchers in New York prepared for the 7:30 A.M. meeting on the 89th floor. A number of people have since remarked how wonderful that last meeting was. Will DeRiso, one of our salespeople, remembers looking around and thinking how great it was that every single analyst, except one junior analyst, was attending that day. This rarely happens, since most times at least a few of the analysts are on the road or at conferences. Will also remembers noting that almost every trader was there as well. The room was packed with between 50 and 60 people attending the meeting that day.

It was a pretty standard day. "Nothing unusual," recalls Bob Planer, who was then a senior vice president on the sales side. We've since promoted Bob to executive vice president and associate director of equity sales. "We were looking forward to getting going again because with summer over, September is usually a really busy month," he says.

The meeting, which had started somewhere between 7:30 and 7:45 had ended around 8:15.

People began to drift back to their offices. As usual, some congregated around the trading desk to joke, catch up on what was going on, and just kid around a little before settling into their daily routine. Some of the salespeople were already at their desks making telephone calls and sending e-mails to their clients about information received at the morning meeting.

That's exactly what Bill Henningson, one of our equity sales-people, was doing when he heard a muffled explosion. Will told me that the building shook as if there were an earthquake. He later found out that the explosion was the plane hitting the first tower. Joe Berry, our chairman, came running out of his office and yelled, "Jesus Christ, what the hell was that?"

Everyone on the 89th floor started to look in the direction of the other tower, which couldn't be seen from our offices on the trading floor. Although the building wasn't visible, our employees could see that the air was filled with paper and a great deal of smoke. (Remember that we were on the 88th and 89th floors and it was rare to see paper that high up.) Bill describes the scene as "almost a confetti parade." Someone yelled that there had been an explosion in Tower One.

Some people got up and ran to the windows to try and see what was going on—but not everyone. The traders remained working at their desks. This might seem strange to those not inti-mately involved in the trading community, but those who know this environment understand. Bill offers this explanation:

The traders sat in their seats doing their jobs because that's what traders do. They need to answer the telephones and complete the trades for customers. Many of the traders are tough, not only the men—the women, too. They don't move until the job is done. They rarely get up, except to use the restroom. That's how it is on all the desks. The traders are very aggressive and are here to do their job.

KBW's equity trading group was led by Frank Doyle. Frank was an executive vice president, member of our operating committee, and a board member. Frank earned his stripes on our equity desk as an arbitrage trader. He often carried the largest positions on our desk and frequently was the most profitable trader in the firm. He was a no-nonsense type leader and our equity business, with Tom Michaud running sales and Frank running trading, enjoyed great success under his tutelage. Even an explosion in the other building didn't change this mind-set.

The situation on the 88th floor was quite different. To begin with, not everyone had arrived. This floor was where most of our investment bankers worked and they tended to come to work later and stay in the office later. Still, a number of people were there when the first plane hit. One of our employees, J. J. Aguiar, moved through the office, screaming at everyone he could find to get out, that a bomb had gone off next door. He succeeded in clearing the floor.

J. J. then yelled up the stairs to Fran Haros, the receptionist on the 89th floor trying in vain to get her to leave. Unfortunately, while he appeared to think it was important to leave the building, he didn't realize how imminent the danger was. We're not sure exactly what happened after he reached the 78th floor. Some reports say he stopped to talk to some people he knew. Others say he went back up the elevator to persuade friends of his at Fuji Bank, his former employer, to leave. Whatever the cause of the delay, it cost him and us dearly. He was the only employee on the 88th floor that morning who did not survive.

Those who did leave their desks on 89 were moving away from the trading floor in an attempt to get a better view of what had happened. It looked to them that the explosion in Tower One of the World Trade Center had hit about 10 stories higher than our floor. At that point, most people thought it had been a bomb although some wondered if it was a plane.

Bob, thinking it had been a plane, got up on a ledge to try to see the aircraft, which he thought should lay below. However, he could see nothing and this didn't make sense to him. He kept thinking that if a plane had hit the building, it would have fallen and there should be debris in the street. Since he used to be on a first aid squad, he thought he might be needed if people in the street and possibly on the plane needed medical assistance. This willingness to pitch in probably saved his life. Before leaving, he picked up the telephone to make a quick call home to let his wife know what had happened.

Bob had been working in the building in 1993 at the time of the first bombing. On that occasion, he had spent six hours with Joe Berry Sr. trapped in an elevator before being rescued. When he got his wife on the phone this time, she said, "I don't like the sound of this. Just get the hell out of the building and out of New York."

He headed for the elevator, intending to return when he figured out what was going on. Before he left, he noted that some of the traders who had remained seated at their desks were urging their peers to get back to their desks and answer the phones that were now ringing off the hook. He passed Mike McDonnell, our Controller, who also served as fire warden. Mike was on the telephone with Central Fire Command. After the call, he planned to tell Joe Berry Sr. that he was going to evacuate the offices. Since he couldn't get Joe on the phone, he started walking over to Joe's office. Right to the end, Mike was doing his job.

Meanwhile some of the senior people who had begun to arrive moved toward Joe's office to confer with him about what to do. Bill remembers Joe standing with his arms by his side trying to decide how to deal with the situation. He thought that it must have been a huge quandary for Joe because when the building was bombed in 1993, the best thing to do was stay put. Those people who went the stairs or used the elevators were in the dark and got rained on by the sprinkler system; it was very smoky and hot. That was probably a factor running through his head. As we later found out, the situation in the stairwells had been rectified and smoke and water were not an issue. However, it is unlikely that Joe knew this.

Our fixed income group suffered terribly on 9/11. Many of the individuals in the office that day were victims—of the 16 employees in that group, only five survived. Thankfully, KBW has great fixed income talent in our regional offices and several seasoned NYC-based fixed income professionals who were not in the office at the time of the attack. This department, terribly brutalized, was able to function post 9/11. For example, on September 11, KBW was about to lead a $100 million bond offering for the largest privately owned bank in the country, First Bank Oak Park. Market conditions and the personal losses we had, caused this deal to be delayed. It wasn't until December that we launched the deal, but we added Lehman Brothers as a co-manager and led the deal to a very successful completion. We sold this deal with only about a quarter of the professionals that we would normally have working on the transaction. Also the firm co-led the largest bond deal in its history in December of 2001. KBW and First Tennessee led a $923 million pooled trust preferred offering. Not only did our group offer fabulous execution, but also an important message was sent to the marketplace that KBW's fixed income franchise could not be ignored.

The fixed income group at KBW has been around almost as long as the firm. It wasn't until the mid-1990s that we started to grow the franchise. The firm has always been strong in research-ing and trading fixed income instruments of banks and thrifts, es-pecially the mid- and small-sized institutions. In the mid-1990s, KBW built a team to focus on building a business where the cus-tomer was the banks and thrifts. This business was all about KBW helping banks and thrifts better manage their assets and liabilities. It was a natural for us and we called this group our financial strategies team. The entire fixed income operation was headed by Joe Lenihan. Unfortunately, Joe was a 9/11 victim. He had been with KBW for 16 years and there were few more dedicated than he. He wore many different hats at the company, and he wore them well. In addition to running fixed income for the firm, he di-rected equity and fixed income syndicate and was one of our biggest producing fixed income salespeople.

The remainder of this chapter depicts the experiences of a few of our employees. I believe these vignettes reflect the caring, fa-milial spirit we have worked so hard to develop at KBW. We have a dual purpose at this company: We strive to be the very best at what we do and we try to take care of each other. This spirit was evident on that terrible day and it is with this same spirit that we are determined to rebuild our company.

Returning to Bob Planer's story, Bob had no trouble getting on an elevator. He says it was crowded but not packed, and he reached the ground floor fairly easily. He then took the escalator to the promenade between the two buildings to find a better vantage point. He describes the scene as eerie as smoke and debris filled the air and people from Tower One fell screaming onto the promenade. As security ushered people out of the area, he says he heard a loud rumble, like a muffled roar. He thought that it was the first tower exploding, never imagining that a second plane would strike.

The security guards were working desperately to keep people away from the falling debris and get them to safety. Bob says he was not scared until he saw the "panic on the face of one of the security guards" trying to clear the devastated areas. He split off from the crowd and finally emerged on Broadway, turning to see that his building was now on fire.

"I was totally shocked at the sight," he said, "I had no phone, no way to call the office." He tried to find a public telephone, but none were working. Given the general panic, the human carnage, and his complete inability to get back in the building, Bob did the only thing possible—he went home. Luckily, Bob commutes via a nearby ferry and was fortunate enough to find one arriving as he reached the station. Deeply shaken, he walked to the ferry's top deck. At just the moment that the ferry was passing the Verrazano Bridge, Bob saw the building that housed our offices, Two World Trade Center, coming down.

A sickening feeling came over him, realizing that he had just witnessed the deaths of his KBW colleagues and friends. He knew that had he been there, he would have gone to the roof. That was everyone's escape plan. No one ever thought the building would come down.

Bob wonders, with admiration, at the split second decisions made by five of our other employees, Andrew Cullen, Will DeRiso, Jeff Hansen, Amanda McGowan, and Bill Henningson. "They are amazing to me," he says. "They just took off without even looking out the window to see what was happening. They heard it and left. Thank God."

When Bill Henningson heard the explosion, he said to himself, "It's a bomb. I'm out of here." He had made a prior decision that if anything ever happened he was going down the staircase. He quickly noticed Will De Riso and Cliff Gallant, another survivor, interacting in the hallway and saw the fear on their faces. He spotted Amanda McGowan, a KBW salesperson, heading for the stairs as well. That was all the indication he needed. What happened next was so harrowing Bill admits that, "the events of the next 18 minutes are in dispute." He doesn't really know what occurred at certain points. From various conversations, however, he has pieced together the following scenario.

A number of KBW people from the 89th floor entered the stairwell at approximately the same time. They broke into pairs and became separated as they worked their way down the stairs. Bill believes that Will and Cliff were ahead of him, at least they started in the stairwell before him and he doesn't remember passing them. However, when the plane hit Tower Two, Will was in the stairwell in the 50s and Bill was on the 44th floor. How did Bill get so far ahead? Bill explained to me that, "Some of the people thought that maybe we went down a lot more stairs and may have gone all of the way to the 44th floor. At that point, we decided that we had overreacted and got in an elevator to go back to the 89th floor and found out that we couldn't go all the way up because of the limited access to floors of certain elevator banks

and came back down again. As a result, we were at another elevator bank when the plane hit."

In the interim period, between the time when the first plane
hit and the second tower was struck, there was a message over the
intercom saying, "Tower One has been hit by an airplane, Tower
Two is secure and structurally sound. Please return to your floors."
Some reports, however, indicate that there was an addendum to
that message indicating that people should return to their floors
unless otherwise authorized by a company representative. Bill
suspects that the intercom message was the impetus that caused
people to try to return to the office. Some people including Bill
believe that on a floor somewhere in the high 70s to low 60s there
was a door open with a guard with a radio urging people to get
out of the stairway.

The 44th floor was one of those huge concourses where you
changed elevators to get to the lobby or reach higher floors including the 89th. It was crowded with people, but Bill, Amanda,
Andrew, and Jeff managed to get into an elevator. Before the doors
closed, there was the rumbling and shaking that we now know was
the second plane hitting our tower. Bill was struck with a piece of
plaster and blown into a wall. He describes it as "inertia—not inertia where you are pushed but like inertia where air lifts and
blows you across a room." He remembers waking up dazed on the
concourse finding himself surrounded by smoke and alone.

He quickly realized that most of the people who had been in
the elevator with him had not gotten out. There was no sign of
Amanda. This upset him greatly.

What he did not realize was that Amanda and Andrew Cullen
were actually ahead of him. When the plane hit, all four in their
group had been on the elevator and Andrew was knocked off his

feet while lunging at the elevator door in an attempt to get off. Managing to exit, Andrew ran down the stairwell to the 43rd floor where he stopped to wait for his colleagues. Within 30 to 40 seconds, Amanda joined him. It was only when they got to the street level that the two noticed the people falling from the building and debris falling.

Meanwhile, still on the 44th floor, Bill stood up and ran to the other side of the floor, normally occupied by Morgan Stanley employees. Out of the smoke ran one of his colleagues, Jeff Hansen. He was so happy to see Jeff that he wanted to hug him. The two stayed together through the rest of the ordeal.

The two men proceeded to walk down the remaining 44 flights of stairs. Even though Bill injured his knee, he said he didn't even notice. The smoke that had bothered him earlier was largely limited to the 44th floor. Bill remembers passing firefighters and other emergency workers in the stairwell, and he noted how kind and polite people were. One man even stopped to lend him a pen so he could jot down Jeff's telephone number in order to contact him after he reached home. The man stopped and waited quietly until Bill had finished writing.

While crossing through the lobby, Bill saw the most incredible sight. A woman was being rushed through the crowd—people accompanying her were clearing the crowd. She had burns over 70 percent of her body. She had a reverse Mohawk because she had been burned across the middle of her head. She was covered with soot, her clothes were burned, her face was ashen—but the one thing Bill remembers most was how she refused to let anyone touch her. She was going to walk out of this place on her own. "She was the bravest person besides the firefighters and the police officers that I saw."

When Jeff and Bill reached the street, they decided to get as far away from the area as quickly as they could. Instinctively, they knew the buildings were coming down. After putting some distance between themselves and the World Trade Center, they tried to call their families. However, like Bob, they had left without their cell phones and found the pay phones in the area were not working. They decided to head for Jeff's apartment on 13th Street where Bill finally reached his family.

Bill's father had been on his way to work when the train he was on was stopped and evacuated, leaving him near the World Trade Center. He had been standing on the street watching when the second plane flew into the building where he knew his son worked. He immediately headed for his wife's office to prepare her for what he thought was the inevitable news about Bill.

Once he arrived home, Bill called John Howard, who runs our Hartford office. Calls like Bill's helped launch Hartford's efforts in creating a central repository of information for our company. Instinctively, John knew his role and began keeping track of our people.

Meanwhile, Amanda and Andrew had reached the health club where Amanda retrieved footwear she had in her locker (she had lost her shoes during her descent) and Andrew attempted to phone one of his brothers. He was on the telephone when Tower Two began coming down. He says the noise was unbelievable. However, even more disturbing than the noise was the flying glass that seemed to come from everywhere. Andrew dove for the wall as people began running into the club. He noted that many were either slightly or seriously injured. Again, he and Amanda had managed to avoid injury. They decided to leave the financial district as quickly as possible. Andrew says that what they saw as they headed east was "like a holocaust." It took them close to an hour and a half to walk to Amanda's Manhattan apartment.

Unlike Bill, Will did not instinctively know that he should leave. He says that changing desks was actually what got him moving in the right direction. Will had switched desks the night before so that he was now closest to the door. He remembers one of his associates joking with him that if something happened, he'd be the first one out. Being closest, he ran to open the door when he heard someone banging on the other side. Two women from the IT department, which was located in the part of our building closest to Tower One, were standing there. They were so scared that they couldn't speak. The fear on their faces said it all. Spotting Cliff Gallant and several others heading for the stairs convinced Will that he ought to leave as well. He quickly followed believing that the rest of the staff was behind him. He recalls that at one point he and Cliff stopped and debated turning back, fearing they had overreacted. Luckily, they didn't.

He, too, remembers hearing the announcement saying that Tower One had been hit but that Tower Two was secure. He believes they were in the stairwell between the 52nd and 53rd floor when this announcement was made. They were still standing there when the second plane struck. He says his first reaction was that the first tower had tipped over and slammed into the second tower. Ironically, that seemed more likely than what had actually happened.

There was a lot of screaming in the stairwell before a few people began yelling for everyone to calm down. Then it became relatively quiet and the two men continued descending. He recalls a man handing out paper towels along the way. The stairwell was becoming smoky and it was hot. The two men walked down 89 flights of stairs. Will guessed that they exited the building by 9:30.

By the time they had reached the street, both buildings were on fire. Will suspected terrorism but had no idea at the time of the cause. Realizing they should quickly get as far away as they could, they began a trek uptown still not knowing what had occurred. Along the way, someone informed them that two commercial airliners had hit the Towers. "At that point it clicked," explains Will. "I was thinking that maybe some of our people didn't have the same reaction we did. Maybe a few stayed. I thought we might have lost 10 to 15 people, if they stuck around."

The two began to run. By the time they got to Cliff's apartment on the Upper East Side, they could barely walk. After reaching the relative safety of Cliff's home, the two men had the same initial reaction as Bill had and phoned the Hartford office. That's when Will first learned how massive our losses might actually be.

We had just hired Jeff Thompson to work in our New York office. He was originally from Hartford and had started on August 29. He was in the restroom when the first building was hit. As he emerged, he heard people screaming in the hallway. He ran into three women who were visibly upset and suggested that they accompany him down the stairs; that they might feel better when they got down. Two took him up on his suggestion.

Ultimately, Jeff walked down the entire 89 flights of stairs. He thinks he was on the 60th floor when the second plane hit our building. He recalls having the strangest thoughts. "I thought I was going to die," he says. "One side of my brain was saying dying sucks while the other side argued back, no, it's okay. Then the first side would chime in, 'No you are really going to die,' but the other side seemed strangely at peace."

His thoughts matched the surreal aspects of the situation perfectly. A little further down, he ran into another woman in the stairwell leaning against the wall having a panic attack. He shook her and urged her to "have her panic attack downstairs." He saw her later on the street and was relieved that she had made it out safely.

Once he escaped the building, Jeff was determined to get off Manhattan Island altogether and ultimately walked over the 59th Street Bridge into Queens, where he called his family. Then he called the Hartford office and was amazed to hear the whole office cheer, although he couldn't understand why. At that point, he didn't think anyone had gotten out and neither did they. The Hartford group was happy to find at least one survivor.

There he was—a guy originally from Hartford, with a temporary apartment a few blocks from the Trade Center, and a family in Darien, Connecticut—stranded in Queens. He wanted to go home, but Queens was entirely in the wrong direction. He realized that to get back to the city he was going to have to walk over another bridge. A policeman introduced him to a visiting nurse who suggested that they pretend he was a patient she was helping in an emergency situation. That would get her, her car, and Jeff over the bridge without walking. She drove him all the way to Darien, Connecticut, where he was finally reunited with his family.

The men were not the only ones who got out in the nick of time. Two of our women had a truly harrowing experience escaping from the building and in leaving the area surrounding the World Trade Center.

Linda Rothemund, a research associate, had just returned from the morning meeting when she heard a loud bang. She turned to look out the window facing Tower One and saw debris and flames. She, too, remembers paper flying everywhere and thinking it must have been a bomb. Along with several coworkers, she headed for the windows to get a closer look. She also recalls the traders working at their desks, almost oblivious to what was going on around them.

Linda and the rest of the research group were still on the 89th floor when the fire marshal made that fatal announcement stating that the first building had been hit but our building was secure. She called her family to tell them she was okay, and then grabbed her bag and joined her work group, Russell Keene, Lauren Smith, and Dean Eberling, to leave.

Linda's and Lauren's group was one of the small groups we had hired en masse. Here's how Lauren describes the team and their process.

> The seventh-year anniversary of Dean and I working together was ironically the Tuesday before 9/11. Thelma had joined the team just a few weeks before me. (Thelma had called in sick that day.) Russ joined us in 1997 while we were at Prudential Securities; Gregg Trost had come on board in 1998 while we were at Putnam Lovell; Linda became part of the "Deanteam" in 2000 at KBW. We were the "Deanteam" . . . Dean was the glue that kept us all together despite all our different but complimentary personalities. We were more than coworkers . . . we were friends and had all experienced many stages of life together, both happy and sad. We were a "lift out" from Putnam Lovell to broaden the research coverage at the firm to include Brokerage and Asset Management and

were thrilled to move to KBW. The firm had a wonderful reputation, a stellar research and sales effort, top-tier investment banking practice . . . and the people . . . well, you could tell it was different and unique. Everyone really, really cared about each other and the collective success of the firm . . . it was a breath of fresh air . . . it was family.

Linda recalls seeing David Berry, the head of research, in the hallway saying, "anyone who wants to call it a day, go ahead." She believes she was still on the 89th floor, 10 minutes after the first building was hit. The rest of the research department was preparing to leave as well.

Meanwhile, Tom Theurkauf was trying to round everyone up and get them out. His refusal to leave until the entire research department had evacuated ultimately cost him dearly. Two of our employees were so upset by what was going on, they literally could not move. Tom stayed telling them he would not leave without them. The rest of the research staff, with the exception of the "Deanteam" waited. Eventually, he got them going, but it was too late.

Linda, Lauren, Russell, and Dean took the elevator to the 78th floor where they had to transfer to another elevator in order to reach the lobby. Linda was surprised that the floor wasn't packed with people leaving. "Normally," she says, "it seems like people wait forever for an elevator on 78, but not this day." Linda said that almost immediately an elevator appeared and they got on. Suddenly the elevator went into free fall. It was later determined that when the second plane hit the tower, it snapped the elevator cable. Everyone dropped to the floor and then miraculously, the elevator stopped. Apparently, the emergency brakes had kicked in.

Linda explains what happened next:

There was no light—the power was out. Our cell phones didn't work. I tried to press the emergency button or the alarm button and the power was out. I don't know how intact our elevator was when it stopped falling. I think the back half of the elevator had kind of caved in. Dean took control asking, "Is everyone okay?" We thought it was probably just a malfunction and that someone would come to get us, realizing that we were stuck.

So we waited maybe five or ten minutes and then flames started coming from underneath us. That was probably from the jet fuel from the planes. That's when we decided we had to get out. We panicked and tried to open the doors. I helped for a while. I remember being basically horizontal and at one point trying to kick open the doors. But then I stepped back because I figured I wasn't as strong as some of the guys. Dean was right up there, in front, trying to open the doors himself. I thought this was it. Russell and I said goodbye to each other. And we all hugged.

I said goodbye to Lauren and Dean as well. They were still trying to open the doors and then somehow I remember seeing some light. The elevator wasn't totally intact because there was some kind of gap between the floor and the doors. I had my shirt over my mouth trying to breathe.

This gap was about eight inches. At first one of the men tried to get through it, but he wasn't small enough. Then it was suggested that Lauren go because she is so thin. However, Linda went first. After some maneuvering, with several of the men lowering her down as far as they could, she jumped and dropped into the lobby. She estimates it was a five-foot fall. She looked around the lobby and there was no one.

Then, someone from the elevator yelled to her. She says she was on a mission, leaping over turnstiles desperately looking for someone to help free her associates. She eventually found some police officers and firefighters evacuating people in the plaza. She yelled to them for help and they came running with their axes and ladders. When she got back, she found Lauren lying injured on the ground. According to Lauren, this is what had happened:

Linda was lowered down, holding on to someone, and she landed safely and ran to the concourse for firefighters and police to come help. I was pushed out and jumped down but caught too much momentum I guess and stumbled forward into the elevator shaft, which was exposed because the elevator was between floors. What broke my fall (about 8 to 10 feet) was a beam—that is how I broke five ribs. I managed to pull myself up by a cable and balance myself while I looked up to see Linda and at least two Port Authority people, I believe. I was screaming for help, they heard me, and pulled me out by my arms . . . it was actually a human ladder of people pulling me out. They carried me out through the WTC concourse first on a huge piece of glass. I was then transferred to a door that they must have pulled off its hinges to use as a stretcher. Linda and I both lost our shoes in the elevator or jumping so she was carried piggyback across Church Street where there were ambulances stationed. We were logged in by paramedics/EMS and there was a priest there, too, and we were put into the ambulance. Linda hadn't suffered physical injuries but we were staying together for support.

The doors to the ambulance were barely shut when we heard and felt an unbelievable explosion. The ambulance was shaking. The South Tower had collapsed but we had no idea. The EMS guy opened the door and we couldn't see a thing. Linda had surgical gloves on her feet that the priest had given her and we told her to get out and find safety. The EMS man said emphatically, "I will not leave you" so I encouraged her to flee. She walked and ran all the way to Queens after recovering a pair of shoes off the street.

The EMS worker put the other woman in the ambulance who was terribly bloodied over his shoulder while he took my hand and led me out. We walked to a Bank of New York branch blocks away where it appeared people were gathering for safety. He said he had to leave us now and go back to help others. I knew I had to leave . . . I didn't feel safe and I could tell something was wrong with me inside. A woman offered to walk with me to New York downtown hospital and I went with her. Somewhere on the street, we ran into two men in FBI uniforms. She left and the FBI agents and I walked together, me barefoot, into the emergency room and then they disappeared. I would think that it was a dream if my friend Dina had not seen me on television with them.

I was stripped and showered down. We were all given masks to wear. It was getting hard to breathe given the smoke and soot. They stitched up my leg, which had been cut. Despite walking all the way to the hospital barefoot, I had only one minor cut on my foot. There was a point at which I remember being left alone and the ER got very quiet. In reflection, I think that is when the second building collapsed.

I was finally taken upstairs for a chest x-ray and taken back to ER in a wheelchair. All of a sudden, a rush of doctors were around me as the pictures revealed I had broken several ribs front and back and that my lung had been punctured and either collapsed or was collapsing. I'm not sure which. Maybe there wasn't time to numb me, because they proceeded to make an incision in my back to insert a tube through my rib cage and into my lung to inflate it. I remember writhing and screaming and I guess I ultimately passed out because the next thing I knew I woke up in a hospital room. Fortunately, the morphine started to do its job.

After many, many tries, I managed to get two telephone calls to go through to friends. My sister lived in San Francisco, and my parents were in Hawaii on vacation. You were lucky to get any calls through, let alone long distance. I left a voicemail for my friend Elissa stating I was alive and at the hospital downtown and to please call everyone she could think of and even managed to rattle off my sister's phone number. I got my friend Kim on the phone, too, and similarly asked her to please pass on the word and get word to my parents. Eventually, we had no telephone access at all.

I was transferred the Thursday after in an ambulance to Lenox Hill where I stayed for another nine days. My friends visited me every day . . . .a group of them even made it down there that night. They are some of the most amazing people you have ever met and I love them dearly. Wet wash cloths over their mouths, dodging barricades and patrols, bringing me clothes and food.

The nurses and doctors downtown were terrific but I knew that I was too close to it all, and the hospital had no air conditioning, no phones . . . .I had to get out. I remember either Wednesday or Thursday morning my bed was moved away from the window and the blinds closed because a building close by was being taken down because it had been damaged and they didn't want me to see it or hopefully not feel the rumble and shake. I was transferred uptown and was accompanied by several of my friends in the ambulance.

That night, I was finally able to make and receive telephone calls. I spoke to my parents for the first time and told them that I was okay although the conversation is very much a blur. I was given a lot of morphine before the ambulance transfer because it was a bit risky to move me with the tube in my lung but I had to go.

I saw my parents and sister for the first time that Sunday after they finally made it back to New York. My aunt and uncle and two cousins live in the city and I was surrounded by dozens of friends who visited me almost around the clock. Phone calls from coworkers, former coworkers, and friends from all over helped to keep me well occupied while the morphine kept me calm. I had no concept of the magnitude of what had happened in reflection. I went on the radio from my hospital bed, 1010 WINS, in hopes of garnering attention for rescue workers to get to the elevator bank in 2WTC because that is where I left Dean and Russ and many others in the elevator and many firefighters. I just had no idea . . .

My lung healed fine after a little setback that kept me in the hospital longer than I would have expected, 10 days in total. My leg was injured when a piece of the elevator wall pinned me down. The second week of October, I had surgery to extract a blood clot in my right leg. I have healed very well overall but my leg is still not right and I will be having another procedure.

I recuperated at my parent's house in Long Island for two months leaving only twice to attend Dean and Russ' memorials, which were in late October and early November. My injuries spared me having to endure the unthinkable emotional drain of attending memorial after memorial like most of my colleagues. My thoughts and prayers were there for each and every one of the precious lives that were lost.

We only have sporadic accounts of what happened to our employees who did not get out. My son, Christopher, last communicated with his brother Kevin, who attended college in Vermont. Kevin had called Christopher that morning on his cell phone when he got news of the World Trade Center attack at school. Somehow, he got through. It was clearly after the second plane had hit the South Tower. Christopher, in a very brief conversation with Kevin, told him that they were in trouble. They were in a stairwell. They had tried to go down but were on their way back up. He said that he couldn't stay on the phone much longer.

We don't really know the exact time of that phone call, but that was the last communication anybody in the family had with Christopher.

A few other families had similar communications. A small number had contact with family members almost to the end via cell phone. This is what we've been able to piece together. Dean and Russell were in the elevator together when the end came. Most, if not all, of our other employees were not alone. There was a group, as my son indicated, in the stairwell. Another group remained in our offices. Our people were together, in small groups, at the end.

As unpleasant as the situation was for Lauren and Linda, that is only a small part of what our people had to deal with in the aftermath of September 11. Many had "survivor guilt" wondering why they got out, why they were spared, when so many others weren't. They wonder "why me?" Some believe they were saved so they could do some good in the future. They wonder what that good is and will they be able to recognize the opportunity when it comes their way.

They have to live with the knowledge that so many of the people they cared for are no longer with us. Moreover, they had front row seats to some of the worst human carnage—something most people in this country will never witness. They watched buildings topple knowing thousands of people were in them, they saw people jumping to certain death to avoid an even more unpleasant fate when flames engulfed the building. They saw the blood and remains in the promenade as they rushed out of the towers.

It should come as no surprise to learn that not all of our people were able to return to work immediately. Each went at his or her own pace, coming in when they could. Ultimately, a few realized that they could not cope with the situation or with remaining in New York.

Lauren summarizes the situation like this: "Life now is different in so many ways. It is a constant struggle to process this horrific situation . . . but you simply find the strength to rise above and move on because there is no other alternative. Every day you go to work and do something meaningful. It is a tribute to all the special friends that we lost."

After 9/11, we quickly realized that we had several jobs ahead of us: the obvious task of rebuilding our fine company; the moral obligation of taking care of the families, especially those with children; and the need to heal and go on. Part II of this book reveals how we accomplished these goals.

TRIUMPH

THE HARTFORD COMMAND CENTER

T he actions of the 12 people at KBW's Hartford office on 9/11 and in the weeks that followed ended the debate as to the importance of maintaining this satellite office. (More than occasionally, the need for this location had been debated, sometimes quite hotly, at the firm—particularly after Gene Bruyette retired in 1991.) For KBW, the people in the Hartford office played a crucial role in helping us move past the tragedy and begin the process of rebuilding our firm almost immediately after the events of that day.

These are selfless people who, when interviewed for this book, quickly denied that what they had done was anything special. One after the other, they protested, "We're not heroes. The real heroes are the firefighters and emergency service personnel who went into the Towers." Without a doubt, the rescue workers are heroes. But, as you will see, our Hartford employees made a heroic effort to aid their KBW family in New York.

The morning started in Hartford as it had in New York. Our folks were watching CNBC in somewhat cramped offices and waiting for the markets to open, having already participated in the morning meeting. The futures were up eight or nine points when suddenly they dropped ten. Seth Miller remembers being on the telephone with one of his clients and noticing the dramatic fluctuation. His immediate reaction was to tell the client that he would find out what had caused such a precipitous drop. Like everyone else at that point, he assumed a bad earnings report or the like had been announced. Terrorism never crossed his mind.

Immediately, Hartford phoned KBW's New York trading floor to see what had happened. They were told that something had exploded in the other building, but at this point, no one realized that there was a plane involved. Some thought it was a bomb, while others conjectured that a steam pipe or something like it had exploded. In Hartford, they were simultaneously watching their screens and CNBC while talking to our New York traders when our building was hit.

They watched it happen; and then their phones went dead and the computers shut down. People sat motionless, not knowing what to think, or say, or do. Then the Hartford staff started moving—trying to locate cell phone numbers so they could reach our New York staff. They realized the plane had hit a floor lower than the one where our offices were located but they still had hope. At first, it was not clear to them that a commercial airline had hit the building. Envisioning a smaller plane, those in Hartford hoped for the best—a fire in part of the building with our people scrambling to safety on another part of the floor. Yes, it might be difficult getting out, but at that point it seemed feasible.

Then the building fell. Silence engulfed the room as those in Hartford realized the inevitable.

With the second building down, it was apparent that the markets would not open that day. Our people tried to figure out what to do next. With little news available as to the cause of the disaster, some felt that the country might be under attack and those in tall buildings under assault. This became a bigger concern as the news about the Pentagon and the downing of the plane in Pennsylvania trickled in. There was some worry that our Hartford office, located in the United Technologies building, might even be a target. In light of the available news, it seemed as though the country might be under attack. Within the office, employees considered the option of going home.

As the staff prepared to leave, the telephones began ringing. First to call were KBW people on the road and those who had not yet reached the office that morning. Then calls came from the few employees who had actually escaped from the building. These were cause for cheering. Jeff Thompson was the first of such calls, and he was stunned to hear the cheers, not knowing the full effect of the attack.

Then the group mobilized. They sent people home that afternoon to get ready for the evening rush. Someone from our office called CNBC and ABC Eyewitness News and gave them the 800-phone number to run on their tape. This provided family members and other concerned parties with a place to call for information. The number given was the one we normally used with customers. But, recognizing the gravity of the situation, our people felt it appropriate to share it and I applaud them for this action.

Thankfully, some of KBW's longest serving employees work in our Hartford office. John Howard, Joe Spalluto, Jim Healey, and Dean Rybeck each have over 20 years of service with the company. They really stepped up when their leadership was needed.

From the earliest moments on, the telephones almost never stopped ringing. Calls were still coming in at 1 A.M. the following

morning and our Hartford people were there to take down information and provide as much comfort as possible to the families of
those who were missing. While most of the staff focused on the
families, a few of the more senior staff turned their attention to
getting the business back up and running.

Why did our Hartford people behave as they did? "For some
reason," explains Andy Granger, "I didn't want to leave. It wasn't
being heroic or wanting to help the families. I just didn't want to
go." Daryle Dilascia further elaborated on these feelings, explaining, "Part of the reason why we stayed was selfish. We wanted to
hear from as many people as we could, hear from friends and colleagues who were missing. During the first 24 hours, some small
percentage of the phone calls received was positive. Someone
would call and say, 'I overslept' or 'I was in the building and I
made it out.' Those were great phone calls to get." Unfortunately,
after that first day, there were no more positive calls.

For the next two weeks, the Hartford group worked 18 to 20
hours each day, taking telephone calls from the families of the
missing and doing the only thing they could—they listened.
They provided support for anyone who needed a sympathetic lis-
tener. Most of the staff pitched in and helped with this effort—
even Hartford's most recent hire, Chris Orszulak. A new college
graduate, Chris had joined the company only one month earlier.
The group was pressed for space in our old quarters and Chris
didn't really have a work area, creating a makeshift desk out of a
few file cabinets. Chris dealt with the families more than anyone
else in the office, because, as he puts it, he was new and didn't
have an established book of business.

In the beginning, some families called many times throughout
the day. It was not unusual in the first day or two to get a phone
call from the same family member seven or eight times, as the

family prayed for some good news or perhaps a miracle. Maintaining the composure and sensitivity to deal with the volume of such calls was an overwhelming undertaking. "We basically took an internal pounding," explained Seth Miller. "We hung up, cried, and then answered the phone again. There was a period when the phones rang nonstop for two days. Every line was lit."

When the weekend came, some of the staff went home—but only after giving their home phone numbers to those families they had grown close to. Eventually, the group accepted the inevitable, but not feeling it was their place to shatter the hopes of the families, they tried to steer family members toward the many resources for locating and identifying the missing that the city had set up.

The group worked hard at assembling information, trying to determine who was where and if it was possible that some individuals escaped. Every detail gleaned from those who were in the building that morning, as well as family and friends who received calls from inside Tower Two, became crucial. Accurately piecing together the event in entirety seemed critical in determining the fate of our employees. Seth had spoken to one mother from out-of-state who had spoken with her daughter after the first plane hit. Her daughter had said that she was leaving the building as soon as she hung up the telephone. Like many other people, this mother started counting. If her daughter had left when she said she was, could she have escaped? The mother hoped that her daughter had left in time and she was coming in with the rest of the family to search the hospitals.

The phone rang in the Hartford office at 4:30 A.M. on the day the family was leaving for New York, waking Seth who remained in the office to manage the phones. Calling was a gentleman from Germany who had seen our Hartford number on CNBC. This

man had met the employee in question that summer at a conference and had called her after hearing the news on 9/11. It was just
a casual friendship, but he wanted to know if she was one of the
survivors. Seth questioned him about the exact time he had made
that fateful phone call. He realized that she had spoken to him
after she had told her mother she was leaving. He also realized
that, this being the case, it was unlikely that the woman had escaped the building.

Learning this, Seth found himself in a quandary about what
to do. Should he let the family go on a futile search for their
daughter or call and advise them to bring a DNA sample? We all
know the right answer, but how many of us could have picked up
the phone at 4:30 in the morning to call a family with such
dreadful news?

Seth made this difficult choice, and the resulting phone call
was one of the hardest he had ever made. Seth connected the
woman's family via conference call with the gentleman from Europe so they could question him. When it was over, the mother
thanked Seth. He remembers sensing her strength and feeling
that she would want to know the truth of the situation. This had
given him solace for making the right decision. This incident
characterizes the types of interactions and bonds that our people
had with many of the families.

The Hartford staff began compiling information about the
New York staff almost immediately beginning with an old phone
list. Within a few days, Josephine Fink, in the New York office,
obtained a list of all of our employees from the payroll service.
Daryle Dilascia started keeping track of the survivors and those
missing on an Excel spreadsheet. This database quickly expanded. He tracked who had phoned from each family and

recorded their phone numbers, promising that someone would call back if there was anything to report. This ultimately became a massive undertaking.

The spreadsheet grew as different information points were added to it, and in its final form contained physical descriptions of the missing. Andy Senchak felt that recording and expanding this information base was crucial. The added turmoil that families of all those missing in the disaster had experienced early on due to misinformation was heartbreaking and our Hartford staff wanted to avoid this under all circumstances. Andy has often told me how proud he was of his colleagues; how they just "sucked it up and did what had to be done." He describes his associate Seth Miller as a "cantankerous type of guy in business with an unbelievably huge heart." He says that Daryle "did a real good job at organizing everything so we knew who was out [of the building] and who was not."

Toward the end of the week, several senior members of the New York staff came to spend the day in the Hartford office, including Tom Michaud, Michael O'Brien, and Mitch Kleinman, the company lawyer. It was at this time, as a result of several encounters that different people had with the survivors, that the Shepherd program was born. On the way to the office, Michael had stopped at the home of one of his friends, Adam Lewis, who was also among the missing employees. He met with Adam's wife Patty and her father. She was trying to go through the family's financial records and didn't really understand them.

"Driving north to Hartford," says Michael, "I realized how many different needs these families would have and conceived of the idea of matching a KBW person with each family . . . to serve as a resource, a go-to person to help answer any questions that might arise. This person would serve as an advisor and comforter and general supporter, a communicator of KBW information that would be helpful to the families."

Several other senior employees were rapidly recognizing the need for such a plan, which is discussed in greater length later in the book.

Eventually, there was another list to be kept. This one fell to Chris Orszulak. It was a list of when each of the memorial services was to be held, along with family contacts. This was used to disseminate information internally if members of our staff wanted to attend the services.

☆ ☆ ☆

The Hartford group received some assistance from surprising sources. As I mentioned earlier, we had overgrown our existing office quarters. Now, with the influx of staff from New York, we were becoming increasingly cramped. Our landlord lent us some extra space to accommodate our guests and the temporary staff assigned to the office. Clients and local restaurants donated food for our people who were working 24/7. They knew the type of work days that our staff was putting in, so at all hours of the day and night pizza and sandwiches from local catering places would just appear.

The group was also surprised to receive flowers from a grateful family. Paula Berry, David Berry's wife, sent the flowers to show her appreciation for the information we were able to provide and the comfort our staff provided in her time of grief. Our people were both touched and impressed by this gesture. Her ability to think of others at what was one of the worst moments of her life was inspiring.

Our folks in Hartford faced yet another bombshell: It was determined that the stock market would reopen on Monday, September 17. The pressure of maintaining the information center, assembling staff, and getting our firm back online forced the decision that KBW would open for trading one day later than the other Wall Street firms. (With the exception of two women who had arrived at work after the Trade Center was hit, we had lost all our trading staff in New York—and the pair were both quite shaken by what had happened to their colleagues. So, we were operating with a very short staff.) Once again, our customers stood behind us.

Andy Granger describes what happened when we opened our doors for business the morning of Tuesday, September 18:

> We got nailed with orders. People know that's how we make money. They trade with us and we earn commissions on their trades. So, they brought us their business en mass. A good day for a trader at our company is perhaps a million shares. We were trading 10 million shares and no one got upset with poor execution. We hustled all day. It was awesome, seeing those orders come in from all different folks.
>
> In our Boston office, where Katie Ré and Courtney Webber, our surviving NYC sales traders, had relocated, over two-thirds of the volume was traded.
>
> Everyone committed themselves to trading. The situation couldn't have been more cooperative. Our desk had never seen volume like this and our people and systems were taxed to the max.

It wasn't easy for our Hartford people to open the doors that Tuesday. They were suffering. They'd lost good friends and had spent a week on the telephones listening to grief-stricken family members. But they knew it had to be done. If the firm were to survive, someone had to start bringing in some business. So, just as they had a week earlier, they did what had to be done.

I'm sure the enormity of what these people have endured has taken a personal toll. Not only did many lose long-time friends and associates, they listened for days on end to the unending grief of the victims' families—many of whom were complete strangers. Our people in New York also handled calls and listened to family members.

The commitment and actions of our Hartford people resonate with the entire staff. Andy Granger later explained to me that when he and his wife initially came to Hartford, they did so because his wife was doing her residency there and they were not necessarily set on staying. Now he says, "We are staying in Hartford because of this job and these good people. I found such a home here." He also says he's proud of the ways in which the company has stepped up to financially support the KBW families who lost loved ones.

Chris Orszulak, our new hire, says he did a lot of growing up and learned a great deal in those first two weeks when he was putting in 18-hour days. He told me that KBW is the kind of place he wants to be a part of for as long as the firm exists, and he has committed himself to helping us rebuild. He explained that the experience caused him to "appreciate things outside the job a lot more. Spending time with your family is something that you take for granted, but this time is now cherished even more." He has come to realize just how very precious life is.

CIRCLING THE WAGONS: THE NEXT FEW DAYS

Tom and Andy really ran the firm those first few days. While I was at home dealing with my family tragedy, Tom and Andy made some critical choices about the course that we were going to take. They began trying to sort out our priorities and decide what we should do next. Tom and Andy generally split up the firm into two parts. Initially, Tom focused on the firm's brokerage business. The immediate need for him was to determine the firm's positions and manage those positions once the markets reopened. Most of our personnel losses came from the brokerage side of the business. Thankfully, corporate finance had not lost anybody, and Andy focused on setting up the firm's machinery that was going to assist our families. Andy also became a spokesman for the firm and he led our efforts to find headquarter space and rebuild IT. While Andy and Tom communicated constantly, they could not have done it without some of our senior people really stepping up.

On September 12, Andy was up at about four in the morning. He headed up 51st Street to St. Patrick's Cathedral, where he met and began talking with Officer John Begin. Andy told the officer what had happened to our people and the two men embraced and started crying. That morning, Andy was probably the first person in church. Over the next long, painful months, Andy continued to visit Officer Begin.

Mitch Kleinman's training as a lawyer immediately kicked in. Instead of sleeping Tuesday night, he made an outline of what he thought we had to do. It covered a range of issues starting with the obvious: Identifying the people who were missing and piecing together what had really happened. He next outlined items such as insurance issues, operational issues, figuring out what our securities positions were, and determining whether we had a company that could go forward or whether we should consider liquidating. He e-mailed his list up to Hartford before driving there the morning of September 12.

He says that the first thing that happened when he got there was a lot of hugging and crying, and then, they focused on his list.

We had gotten the word out to the employees to come to Wachtell if they felt they were able to deal with the situation. No one was told that they had to come, just whoever could or wanted to. Bernie Caffrey, who had stayed in the city overnight, was the first person to show up. It was really important to see him because we needed to discuss how to take care of our financial positions and related matters. Although, Andy and Bernie felt like they had been washed up on the shores of Wachtell's 38th floor, they started working.

On September 11, luckily Bernie had arrived at work a little later than normal. He was a few blocks away when the building collapsed and had fled from the smoke and dust. Mercifully, we only lost one man in his department, and the rest of his group relocated temporarily to Pershing, our clearing broker across the river in Jersey City. We needed to deal with both our customers' accounts and our own investments, the profit-sharing plan we manage for our employees. It was difficult to figure out where we stood since we didn't really know the full impact of the disaster. We didn't know what cash we had, or what we were facing.

Because we used Pershing to clear our trades, Bernie was able to download all sorts of information from his home. Over the course of that first week, he was able to tell us exactly what we did and did not have financially. Through an odd set of circumstances, including the poor market the weeks before the attack, our traders were very cautious and our positions were much smaller than normal.

By this time, Bernie was working closely with Tom Michaud and John Ragan, who had been appointed interim head of trading.

By the time Bernie sorted through it all—and he literally did this at home over the course of a couple of days—he had concluded that we had about $80 million in cash and a net position of $40 million in highly liquid securities. Additionally, we had about a $15 million receivable coming from our insurance company. When you added it up, if we had closed the doors that fateful day and distributed everything to the shareholders, nobody would have had a loss—which is pretty amazing.

After all that had gone wrong, good news was pretty scarce the first few days. Bernie's analysis was particularly welcome because it meant that we were going to be able to make the *right* decisions rather than decisions made from an incredibly defensive position of trying to protect against major losses. We knew that we had the cash both to pay out to the families of people we had lost and to rebuild the company. Knowing this helped ease our minds. Money, at least, was one less thing to worry about. Tom and John were in charge of managing the firm's positions during that first week.

Bernie wasn't the only person working out of his home to rebuild our company. Remember our IT folks? They converted their townhouse into KBW's interim IT center. As emotionally devastated and overwrought as they were, they knew they had a tremendous task ahead of them—and they stepped right up to do it. They actually rebuilt our network function in their home. They had equipment delivered, went and picked up other needed material in their own cars, and began putting our servers back together.

They had no formal plan to guide them. We had people all over New York City and there was no end to what we needed, including new telephone lines for everyone. The IT folks have been working seven days a week for months just to keep us in some sort of shape. In those first few days, they provided us with the second bit of positive news. Since they had backed up our network the week before, we had lost only one week of data. Luckily, an audit the firm had conducted a short while before 9/11 had revealed that KBW back-up tapes had been stored in a vault in the World Trade Center. Thankfully, we changed this and the tapes were stored at a remote location.

While our Hartford office played an invaluable role those first terrible days, compiling lists and operating the telephones, Andy quickly realized we had another problem. We were swamped with calls from the families. We had to get to organized, figure out how to talk to them. Then he remembered. We know how to take care of people. When you think of it, that's our business. We take care of our clients. What we had to do was shift our thinking slightly so that we could help the families. Therefore, we said okay, we have to link each family with someone senior in the firm to contact about their feelings, needs, and what we could do for them. Since most of us had worked together for so many years, such assignments seemed almost natural. Joe Spalluto and Bob Stapleton were put in charge of this effort.

This idea formed the basis for what was to become our Shepherd program. Unless someone had a distinct reason for picking certain people, we divided the families randomly. In a few cases, a family asked for a particular senior staffer to be their Shepherd. Of course, we honored those requests.

Another list we compiled in those first few days was the record of our employees still missing. On the morning of September 12, there were 68 people on that list. During the day, we heard from a new employee in our mailroom who, being recently hired, didn't realize the significance of our Hartford office and didn't know many people at the firm, and thus, hadn't called anyone. Gratefully, we crossed his name off that fateful list. His name was the only one we were ever able to remove. Within 36 hours, we had identified all the missing.

Our accounting folks ended up at KPMG temporarily, and the tragedy struck them particularly hard. We'd lost our CFO, Jeff Fox, and controller, Mike McDonnell—two much loved leaders of our accounting staff. At KPMG, the accounting staff worked on their laptops sitting around a big table in a small conference room located in the southwest corner of the building that was filled with new papers and boxes. The sun streamed in. Anyone who has worked in a big office building exposed to sunlight knows that this can be more of a curse than a blessing. As the temperature soared in the afternoon, our people endured the heat and did what they had to do to get our accounting function back in shape.

Disseminating accurate information about our people became a priority early on. After Andy and I spent that Tuesday afternoon reviewing the status of our personnel—which was our major focus until it had been definitively determined exactly who had been in the building, who had been seen, and who we knew was safe—we concluded that we needed to make our findings public. We quickly made the decision to put the information on our KBW company Web site so that those concerned about an employee's safety had an authoritative source to go to for that information. We learned that some of the Web sites that encompassed all of the different firms and people who were in the Trade Center contained incorrect information, which ultimately caused confusion and additional grief.

The next issue to unexpectedly surface was dealing with the media. We've always been a private firm and rarely had much to do with the press. However, suddenly we were barraged with requests for interviews. A year earlier in October 2000, we had hired Trimedia, a corporate public relations firm, to promote one of our research products because while KBW may have been a household name within the Wall Street Community, we needed to increase general public awareness of our name. Although the firm did other things for us, its primary task was getting our research product in front of more eyes and raising the profile of some of our analysts with strong records of accomplishment.

Our account manager at Trimedia is Neil Shapiro. When he heard the news, he immediately began trying to get in touch with us, and eventually, he was able to get through to our Richmond office, but they had no idea who he was. On the morning of September 12, he reached Hartford and spoke to Mitch Kleinman, who told him the bad news. Most of the people Neil had dealt with were missing. Neil offered Trimedia's services and suggested that any media calls be directed to him. He provided his home phone, cell, and work numbers so he could be reached 24/7. The idea was to funnel all calls from the media through Trimedia to ensure that accurate information was provided at all times—often much easier said than done as reporters peppered some of our people with calls at home.

Once we had made the decision to rebuild, which we did almost immediately, we realized that we needed to get the message out. Even before I returned to work, Trimedia sat down with Andy, Tom, and Mitch to work out the specifics. Our priority was the families, but we needed to let the world know about our commitment to carry on.

Since most of our remaining people were working long hours trying to provide information and a willing ear to the families of the missing, we had limited resources and decided to focus on the business press. Thus, after some gut-wrenching deliberations, we turned down invitations to appear on the *Barbara Walters Show*, the *Today Show*, and numerous others.

Instead, Andy appeared on CNBC to deliver our message, to tell about our grief, and our focus on determining those accounted for and those missing—and to emphasize that we intended to rebuild our firm. Going on television to answer questions was definitely not his favorite thing to do, but it had to be done. Like the rest of us, he was grateful for the opportunity to get the word out about our company.

We were also interviewed for an article in *Business Week* for which Andy and Tom provided most of the information. When I returned to the firm, I interviewed with Bloomberg, the *Hartford Courant*, and the *Wall Street Journal* as well as appearing several times on CNBC. I was most appreciative of the time allotted to me before the two days in October when we allocated all our revenues to the KBW Family Fund. Part of our success on those days can be attributed to our ability to publicize the event on CNBC.

Trimedia continued to work with the press. Neil says that for every interview we did, we had requests for another 15 or 20. While we would have loved to talk to all the reporters who wanted to cover our story, we simply did not have the time or people available to do so. However, Neil was able to brief the reporters and provide accurate information. He would verify each request about our staff with Robin Bell in our Hartford office. He says he is amazed because no matter what time of the day or night he called, Robin was always there.

People gradually started drifting in to Wachtell during those first two weeks. After Bernie, there was Mary Johnston, our long-time compliance officer. Next came Paula Scantlebury. Originally from Guyana, she had been on the 88th floor and had grabbed her purse and headed for the door when she heard the first commotion. Most of us did not know Paula that well before 9/11. She took care of the kitchen, ordered supplies, got lunches together, and generally tidied up. On the morning of the eleventh, she had been with us for about a year and a half. When she heard we were convening at Wachtell, she just showed up and went to work.

"I started answering phones," she explains, "because they needed somebody to do it."

Paula stayed for over 10 hours that first day and just kept coming back. She says that she felt it was just something she had to do. It seemed nothing special to her but it touched our hearts. We needed help and she gave it. She had clearly been implanted with the KBW DNA.

Andy was particularly impressed by her, since he was the main recipient of her work. He has since promoted her to office manager for facilities, and on Mondays and Fridays she works with him, taking his calls, making his appointments, and doing whatever else needs to be done.

On Thursday we knew for sure who was missing and who was safe. Once we had a fairly clear picture, it became obvious that the entire equity-trading desk in the New York office, with the exception of Courtney Webber and Katie Ré, was missing. While we were still hoping there might be survivors, it did not look very encouraging. Besides the equity trading desk, among the missing were a couple of equity salespeople, several people from our fixed income division, and virtually the entire bank stock research/equity research department, headed by David Berry and Tom Theurkauf.

It was clear to us that the trading and research operations had been the hardest hit. But despite the decimation in these vital areas, Andy Senchak, Tom Michaud, our director of equity sales, and I were of one mind. We were not going to throw in the towel.

Many organizations outside the firm quickly offered to help. Mitch got a call over the weekend from a representative from the New York Stock Exchange, Joe Fano. Although visibly shaken by what had happened, he was calling to introduce himself and tell us that the Stock Exchange was going to do everything it could to help us out. He was our liaison with the Exchange and we have him to thank for the fact that we are in as strong a position as we are today regarding regulatory compliance.

Given our mental state, we may not have been thinking very lucidly about our future and couldn't have imagined the job in front of us. But instinctively, we all knew that those who didn't survive the attack of 9/11 would have wanted the rest of us to rebuild the firm, no matter how big the job might be. We realized right from the start that in terms of capital—we would be okay although the people who perished on 9/11 owned a substantial piece of the company. The firm had always been well capitalized and I think intuitively the three of us felt that we had more than enough capital to handle the enormous chore in front of us. Later, when the numbers were added up, we learned that we were correct in our belief about the financial strength of the firm.

How we would rebuild the firm and where we would start was unclear at that time. Simply trying to deal with the shock and sorrow was overwhelming. During most of those early days, I was unable to think about any business subject. It was impossible. I was trying to deal with my own grief and be a source of some comfort and solace for my wife and my four remaining children.

One of our concerns was where we might house some of our people when we did get back in business. Andy, who had been giving a deposition at Wachtell Lipton on that Tuesday morning, made the decision that some of the staff would be housed in Wachtell's offices. BNP/Paribas had some extra space in their offices in the Equitable Building on Seventh Avenue, and generously offered the space which Tom accepted as a place where he could initially place the equity and fixed income salespeople and traders.

Instinctively, we all wanted to have some sort of a prayer service. During those first few days, many were still hopeful. We decided to hold it on Sunday, September 16, 2001. Initially, Mitch's wife, Maggie Ferguson, contacted the archdiocese of New York on our behalf to see if we could have our service in St. Patrick's Cathedral. They said yes, but then for obvious reasons, expanded the service to include all companies. Initially, we intended to participate—after all, our saga was part of the much larger story. Then we started to receive feedback from the families saying that they wanted their own service, which seemed to make a lot of sense.

We wanted a church within walking distance of the Helmsley Palace, where we planned to have a reception after the service. The church needed to be large enough to hold all of the families as well as our friends, associates, and others. We didn't really know how many people to expect. Our estimates ranged from a low of 200 to a high of 800.

Peter Wirth handled the whole thing wonderfully. He booked Fifth Avenue Presbyterian and one of its ministers, The Rev. Dr. J. Oscar McCloud, the assistant associate pastor. However, since many of our employees are Catholic, we wanted to have a representative from the Catholic Church. Mitch's wife called my high school alma mater, Cardinal Hayes in the Bronx, and spoke to the Monsignor John Graham, the current principal. He consented at once to come and speak and asked if he could bring the retired principal from my school days, Monsignor Victor Pavis.

Peter worked hard organizing the service, planning what was going to be said, choosing the hymns, and selecting the readings from both the Old and New Testament. We must have driven the folks at Fifth Avenue Presbyterian a little crazy while we were trying to organize this event. First, we asked to use the church and they agreed. Then as the debate swirled around in our shop, a decision was made to participate in the ceremony at St. Patrick's after all, so Peter had to call the church back and decline their kind offer. Then, the mood swung again and Peter called again. This all occurred on Friday and Saturday morning. The church was most understanding of the stress we were under and agreed a second time to hold the ceremony for us.

The staff at Wachtell created the program for the service and had it professionally printed. Wachtell people also served as ushers at the service. Despite our last minute changes, we somehow managed to get the word out about both the timing and the location of the service. The turnout was overwhelming. Almost two thousand people attended including former employees, customers, clients, and friends.

Unfortunately, there were a couple of people that we were unable to reach. The following night, Mitch received a call from one of our former employees, Roz Walrath, sobbing that she hadn't known about the service until she got back from her weekend house in the Hamptons. She was heartbroken to have missed the service.

The press, for the most part, showed some discretion and honored our request for privacy. The few hard-core newsfolk who did show up were handled by Mitch and Seth Miller. It was a wonderful service and, for many of us, it started the healing process.

Nearly everyone who came to the service went on to the reception at the Helmsley Palace. We completely took over the hotel. Their staff was only prepared for 300 or 400 people. The head of catering, Kathleen Kenney, who had set up the affair, came frantically looking for Mitch. "I need you to talk to this guy," she said. "He's freaking out." She had with her a representative from the hotel who was concerned about providing food that had not been authorized.

He said, "Look, I just need somebody's sign off that you're going to cover for this and to say what you want us to do."

Mitch said, "We're going to pay for it. There's no issue here. Do whatever you need. If you want, I'll hand you my corporate credit card."

The Palace didn't take his card. They trusted us; they simply wanted a sign off that it was okay to feed the hordes of people who showed up.

Mitch said, "As far as I'm concerned, as long as there's somebody here for this thing and you still have food or liquor in the place, just keep serving it."

And they did, managing to make the necessary adjustments to meet our needs. The reception went on for a long time. It seemed like we fed all of New York City. The bill for the food alone was $200,000. Although the day was emotionally draining, it was worthwhile. Unfortunately, it was just the first of many painful steps of healing.

I stayed home taking care of my family for almost two weeks, talking to Andy and Tom every day. I was comforted by our conversations since we were still unsure as to where we stood. In those first couple of days, it was not at all clear when the market would reopen. It was a day-by-day proposition and, frankly, we were hoping the market would stay closed for some period. Though that's not healthy for the markets generally, each day the market remained closed gave us one more day to plan in terms of how we would reopen when the moment came.

I believe it was Thursday, September 13, when the New York Stock Exchange announced that the market would remained closed through Friday and reopen on Monday, September 17. Tom and the others had planned that some of our personnel would go to either the Boston or Hartford office, and we would attempt to do our listed trading business from there when the market reopened.

Given the world events, it was apparent to everybody that there would be enormous volume on opening day, and it was anyone's guess where the stocks would trade. We made the determination late that first week that given how understaffed we were and how we would be trading out of our Boston office with reduced capability, we would take an extra day. We felt it was better for us and for our clients that we not be back in business that first Monday.

Before we started any trading again, all related issues had to be worked out. The IT people did heroic work with Joan Feldman and Rich Fehler riding an emotional roller coaster. They had these enormous swings from worrying about our suffering to dealing with data lines and computer systems. It is almost incomprehensible to me that they were able to get so much work done. Maybe it's those people who said, "I'll think about this later I've got to take care of things now" who got us through. Luckily for us, they were there.

Thus, as planned, we reentered the market on Tuesday, September 18, 2001. That day and for a period of several weeks, we traded only stocks that are listed on the New York Stock Exchange and other Exchanges. We did not attempt to do any market-making activity or trade in the over-the-counter market.

☆ ☆ ☆

My wife and I had gathered our other four children so we could get through this crisis and tragedy together. Two of them, Caitlin and Brian, were already at home and the other two returned home from college on September 11. Two of my daughter Kara's friends drove her home from the University of Rhode Island that afternoon, mere weeks after she had begun her freshman year, and our son, Kevin, drove himself home that afternoon arriving in the evening.

Thus, by nightfall, September 11, 2001, every member of the Duffy family was home—except for one. That first week was the hardest period to get through. There was a feeling of complete numbness at times. How could your son and so many people that you knew for so long possibly be gone? It was and is incomprehensible. I have never had to deal with the multiple deaths of people close to me. As the days went by, it was clear that the odds of anyone having survived the attack were extremely small.

Initially, everyone held out some hope that the folks near and dear to them might have somehow lived. However, as time passed without any rescues, the hope became dimmer and dimmer. My wife and I were struggling with exactly when to accept what was rapidly becoming the inevitable: We had lost our son Christopher.

Attending the funeral of one of our neighbors from Crestwood, New York, helped us with our decision. Although we had not known William Wik well, we attended his memorial service on September 19 at our church, Annunciation Church. His wife and family had decided it was time to have a service for William (who had worked for another firm). The service was extremely well done and a true testament to his life. It helped Kathy and me accept the fact that we needed to do something to bring some closure to our own situation. We felt that our other children, Brian, Kevin, Caitlin, and Kara, needed to begin the painful grieving process.

Therefore, we decided that we would have a wake although Christopher's body had not been found. We held it Friday, September 21, at a local funeral home, McGrath's in Bronxville, New York. The following day, Saturday, September 22, a memorial mass for Christopher was held. Both events were attended by an extraordinary number of people who offered support, solace, comfort, and anything else they could. Support and comfort from friends and relatives overwhelmed us; many childhood and college friends and buddies of Chris, some of whom he had known for almost his entire life, participated.

Everyone was enormously affected by this tragedy and wanted to be part of a the grieving and healing process. The support of those people was critical to my family and me in being able to get through this very rough period. You rely on your faith and you rely on each other to get through something like this. However, the support of friends and relatives was enormously beneficial, helping us remember the good times that we had with Christopher and celebrating his life.

While we were dealing with our own situation, other families were also dealing with the loss of their loved ones and were holding services. If I could have, I would have attended every one of them. Unfortunately, I was not able to attend many. In fact, the memorial for my co-CEO and chairman of KBW, Joe Berry Sr. was held the same day that we had scheduled our service for Chris. I regret not being able to attend Joe's service and many of the others, as well. The firm tried to make sure that in addition to our Shepherd program, we would be well represented at all of the memorial services for our people.

Finding the proper balance between family responsibilities and professional obligations, especially for a CEO, is not easy. I did what I believed was right. Andy recently commented on the way I handled my dilemma. Here's what he said. "John has come back. He did the correct thing. He stayed home with Kathy for two weeks. He took the time to do it. He took care of himself. Then when he came back, he was ready to be back. That was the smartest thing he could have done. Because I think when he did come back, he was here. He had done what he had to do to get himself ready. Moreover, I think he did a good job. I mean, it was time for reinforcements, and I was happy to see him." I returned to work on Monday, September 24, two weeks after the devastation.

There was no trading for the balance of that first week, although I had phone conversations with Andy, Tom, and others during that time to try to talk through some of our operational issues. Where would our remaining staff work? As previously noted, our corporate friends pitched in offering space at BNP for the equity team, housing for our accounting people at KPMG Peat Marwick, and room for our back office or trading support personnel at Pershing in Jersey City. Our asset management people were at Prime Brokers, yet another location.

In addition, our corporate finance people were working out of the offices of Wachtell Lipton. Thus, many of our phone discussions that first week concerned how to make those different locales as operational as we could in a very short period.

Although Tom had accepted the offer of the space on BNP's trading floor, the space still had to be wired with phones, computers, and other equipment so that our traders could trade. Our salespeople, however, were able to work out of the BNP space. The work for the traders' space was not completed until early December. In the interim, the surviving traders continued to work out of Hartford and Boston. They finally came home at Thanksgiving. It was a long temporary assignment, and no doubt a difficult added stress to our already traumatized employees. But they did what needed to be done. Al DiAntonio, one of the alumni we hired back almost immediately, describes his routine during his weeks in the Boston office:

It became routine. I had a four o'clock pickup on Monday mornings to go to the airport. I needed to be on the first shuttle out of Newark to be at my desk at a quarter to eight. Then I'd come home on Friday nights after the market closed. It worked just fine. I grew to really appreciate the decision I had made to be there and was not worried about the sacrifices but just committed to the project of survival and success. I realize we haven't met all our goals but we are getting there. When people ask me how we are doing, I tell them that we take a lot of baby steps and most of them are in the right direction. We're not perfect, but the majority of our decisions have been productive. I am thrilled to be back and hope to stay for the duration of my career.

When we finally resumed trading on Tuesday, September 18, 2001, we took a team approach to covering accounts. Everyone just ran with it. It was a survival mode during the six and a half hours the market was open. When we made our calls, we had two purposes: The first was to do the best we could to execute customer orders, and the second was to act as unofficial PR spokespeople for the firm. We were letting the world know that we were back in business and here to stay. We persevered, whether in New York, Hartford, or Boston.

In the days following the attack, Wall Street was very generous to us, but the reality was that we had to stand on our own two feet. As the Darwin principle of the market kicked in, we had to earn our way, not rely on the sympathy of others.

YOU ARE ONLY AS GOOD AS YOUR EMPLOYEES

The hardest issue we had to face after 9/11 concerned our employees. From the start, it was very apparent that the two departments that had been most impacted by the disaster were our equity trading desk and our research department, primarily the banking industry research division. In fact, virtually our entire bank research staff had been wiped out. Our insurance research division was not as adversely affected, although we did lose one of our fine insurance analysts, David Graifman.

When Tom, Andy, and I met in the early days following 9/11, we made the determination—or came to the conclusion—fairly intuitively that having lost 67 people, it would be impossible for us to try to interview for all those positions at once. Given the number of people we'd have to see to staff those positions, there was no way we could keep all the information flows straight. We didn't have enough hours in the day to contemplate that many interviews in a short period. We discussed our options with some of the other senior people and reached an obvious conclusion: What we needed to do first was rebuild the equity research department.

Equity research has been what KBW has been best known for throughout its almost 40-year history. We began to draw up a list of analysts at different firms who were following the banking industry, and people at buy side firms who we thought might be appropriate candidates. Tom began to solicit suggestions and recommendations from clients and customers on the buy side about analysts at different firms who they held in particularly high regard.

We took the information that we'd gathered and compiled an initial list that contained 40 or 50 names. After talking with our clients and customers, we then prioritized our listings and came up with a shorter list of 20 or 25 names to which we wanted to speak.

Tom and some of his senior salespersons began trying to contact those prospects and arrange dates to meet and interview. In addition to the individuals that we contacted, there were also a number of research analysts who contacted us interested in joining our research effort at KBW. When asked if I was offended by these offers coming so soon after we had suffered such a devastating blow, I replied I didn't have the luxury of taking offense. I ran through a wide gamut of emotions during those first few months, but being offended was never on the list.

Proper etiquette, when coming for an interview at a company that had gone through what we had been through, was not something that is taught in business school. Most people didn't know what to say to us; our interviews were certainly different than anything they had ever encountered before. The candidates felt compelled to say something about being sorry about the losses that we had experienced. Many of them, especially on the research side, knew their counterparts at KBW from conferences and meetings they had attended over the years and, in some cases, they were friends of the missing people. As a result, the opening moments of the interviews were fairly awkward, not only because of the emotional issues involved, but because we were pressed for time and often had several people interviewing one candidate simultaneously.

During these meetings, we were looking for an additional feature on which we might not normally have focused. As always, we wanted to be sure that the people we hired fit in well with the people we already had on board. However, we also needed to hire positive, optimistic people with good attitudes who might lift our morale when our spirits fell.

While we were beginning our restaffing effort, Michael Corasaniti, a former client at Neuberger Berman who had recently joined the faculty at Columbia Business School, was searching the Internet for friends' names to see who had survived and who had not. When he got to the KBW site, he immediately checked for the people who had covered his account at Neuberger. When he discovered that both Mike O'Brien and Amanda McGowan, with whom he had been the closest, had survived, he let out a sigh of relief. However, as he reviewed the list of our missing, he was stunned to realize that virtually everyone else he knew, even slightly, at the firm was gone. In moments, he realized the horrible truth we were facing and said, "Oh my God, they lost all the research department."

He kept saying it over and over again; he was so overwhelmed. I'll let him explain what happened next:

It was really weird. I was sitting there and all of the sudden, the only analogy I can make is that it was like I got a phone call from God, a voice in my head said to me, "Mike, you have to go help." It was so intense that our country was under attack for the first time,

I felt we had to stop the destruction. I kept saying to my wife, "Without a research department, there will be nothing for the survivors. They aren't going to be able to support themselves. The families of the survivors who have stock in the company are not going to be able to get their money out." All of the lives would be impacted even beyond the unbelievable emotional loss.

I didn't even know how to get in touch with anyone. So, I sent Amanda and Mike an e-mail saying if you get this, here's how to get in touch with me. I want to come in and help. My background is rather varied. I've been a salesperson and a trader, I know how to clear trades, write research, and manage money. Basically, I said, "I'm not looking to be paid; I'm a freebie." If you need to close out positions, I can do that. If you want me to write research, I can do that. If you need help clearing in the back office, I can do that. Just tell me when and where to show up.

Michael was at Columbia only part-time and had joined with several friends to start a consulting business. He was mistakenly under the impression that KBW, like some other Wall Street firms, was thinly capitalized and believed we would not have the money to pay him. What he offered, he offered free.

The more he thought about working for KBW, the more excited he became. He realized that he would bring his "whole gang" with him. Since they already had a product, he thought it would be a nice "plug-and-play" fit and that he could jump-start our organization by bringing his whole group along. He was so excited about the prospect that he volunteered his people after talking to only one of his associates.

Mike had gotten hold of Amanda's telephone number and had called her making his offer to help. About 10 days after the attack, Amanda returned his call inviting him to come in and meet with Tom and Bob Planer. He recalls that first meeting in the borrowed BNP space. Most of our trading staff was in Boston and Hartford because the BNP space was in the process of being rewired for our trading; only eight of the two dozen desks allotted to us were occupied. Mike remembers how stark it looked and that the meeting was intense. His first thoughts were of his missing predecessors, Dave Berry and Tom Theurkauf.

Bob asked him if he would be interested in being director of research. It had never dawned on Michael that we might have this in mind. He had never managed people and said so immediately. Bob challenged him to describe how he would operate if he was research director. To Mike, this gauntlet was more than an interesting interview question. At Columbia Business School, when he lectures about security analysis, he uses a case study that is about how he would train people if he were the director of research at a securities firm.

He gave Bob a synopsis of his lecture concluding with the fact that what he had told him was a theoretical blueprint but he emphasized that it had never been put into practice. Impressed, Bob asked Michael if he would be willing to cover stocks as well as be the research director as David Berry had previously done. He said, "I knew David well. He was one of the smartest people on the planet. I can't do that. Either I'm going to cover stocks or I'll be the research director, but I can't do both."

Mike respected Dave Berry enormously. He uses a book given to him by Dave in the classes he teaches at Columbia University— *Common Stock* and *Uncommon Profits* by Philip Fisher (New York: John Wiley & Sons, 1996).

Michael's experience was not a typical KBW interviewing procedure, but what the firm felt it had to do to get the hiring process moving along. A few days later, Michael was invited back for a second interview with the senior executives. Michael and six KBW executives, including Bob Planer, Andy, Tom, John Howard, Michael O'Brien, and I met for a three-hour meeting.

Michael had been through this kind of routine before when working as an analyst at Neuberger, He claims that at Neuberger, though, there were 30 people grilling one analyst, so our six on one wasn't intimidating at all. He does say, however, that the level of the emotion at our meeting was a little different than at his Neuberger meetings, given what we had been through.

By now, Michael had made up his mind that if he joined the group, he wanted to bring his associates from the consulting firm, Jeff Spetalnick and Vincent Daniel, with him. He was still under the impression that the firm was thinly capitalized. During the meeting, he said, "You guys are asking me to be research director. I will tell you how I would do it, but you'll need to interview a few other people who are also interested."

He was talking about his partners, Jeff and Vincent, who we would interview later. However, before we made our final decision regarding Michael, we had some additional questions. In some respects, the research director's position was the most important one we had to fill. He would be responsible for hiring a number of additional employees. We had to make sure that he fit with our corporate culture.

We had many philosophical questions to ask him. We wanted to know what he thought about the investment process; how he would construct the department. There were some things that were very important to Michael and he wanted to make sure that he would be able to implement these principles. For starters, he was concerned about the integrity of the research. He didn't want any meddling from investment banking, as sometimes happens at other firms. We were 100 percent in agreement on this issue. Such a Chinese wall has been a cornerstone of our corporate culture.

He also felt that it was important to allow analysts to change their minds. Let's face it, it happens. He wanted assurances that we would protect our analysts under such circumstances. At many places, this is simply not the case; to Michael, that was a sacrosanct issue. Again, we agreed with him on that one.

Last, he felt it important that we put our analysts out in the regions. He wanted them to see the banks in their local economies. He believes that you learn about local economies by being in the field, interacting with local people with local contacts who can get good information because they are part of the community. He did not want all the analysts living in New York. So, our New England analysts will be in Hartford, our West Coast analysts are in San Francisco, and we will probably have a few people in Chicago covering the Midwest. Of course, they all visit the New York office on a very regular basis.

Because Michael has worked at several different places, he's seen a number of different corporate cultures and practices. He's selected the best practices from each and we plan to integrate them into a truly wonderful team.

We had Michael back for a third meeting, giving him a few hours notice and at the end of that get-together offered him the position of research director. He was pleasantly surprised to discover that the firm is conservatively run and we were prepared to weather the disaster, at least from a financial standpoint. Michael points out that very few investment banks are prepared for an eight standard deviation event. He says he was amazed that his generous offer to work free was not necessary. We wouldn't hire him just because he was free; we hired him because he was good.

Finally, he had one last condition. He wanted to bring in his two partners. He insisted that we meet them before he "officially" accepted the position. Our early press releases indicated that we had hired someone but would delay making the announcement for a few days. It was in that period that we first met Jeff and Vincent.

Because Michael was confident that we would like them, he unofficially accepted our offer and began working immediately. Interviewing concurrently with Michael was a KBW alumnus, Larry Vitale, who had left KBW in the early 1990s and made a name for himself at Bear Stearns and other shops where he had been on the buy side and had run a hedge fund. After meeting with Larry, we decided very quickly that we wanted Larry to be part of the team, whether in research or some other position.

We really felt that we should hire them both. Michael would be director of research. As for Larry, while his title might be uncertain, we knew that with his capabilities and experience, he could help us and our clients make money. We envisioned him as one of our proprietary traders or an investor of the firm's capital. He accepted this role and continues to fulfill these functions. He is excellent at facilitating communications between the equity trading desk and the research effort in terms of exchange of ideas and researching different companies.

Michael and Larry were two of our initial hires, but our very first hire was Al DiAntonio. As noted, Al traded equities for us in the 1990s before he left to join Knight Securities. When we first started having conversations about rebuilding the staff, Al's name came up. Although he was anxious to rejoin us and help, he was initially reluctant to contact us until it was mentioned to him that we might be interested. When Bob told him that his name had been raised as someone we could use, he said, "I'd love to help. Let's talk and make it work."

That's just what we did. I don't think he even came in for a formal interview. He had some telephone conversations with John Ragan, who was now our interim head of trading and Tom Michaud and that was it. He got on a plane and went to Boston for nine weeks until we got our interim trading operation up and running on the BNP trading floor.

John Ragan had gone to college in Boston and always wanted to return. He had long made his wishes known in that regard. If we were to open an office in Boston, John wanted to work there. In the fall of 2000, John was diagnosed with cancer. This was a serious blow to all who worked on the trading desk. John now says there was a silver lining for him in this ominous cloud. We were all worried about him. The people who worked with him, fearing that perhaps he would not make it, all told him how much they cared about him. In a bizarre turn of events, he got to say good-bye to those he worked with and cared for so much, while the rest of us did not.

We decided to open the Boston operation while John was on medical leave. Knowing his wishes, we held open the position to run the operation for him. He returned to work in the beginning of September 2001 and was there to help us when we really needed it.

Another alumnus, Phil Cuthbertson, came back to help us. Phil had left us in the spring of 2000, for lifestyle reasons. He had been with us for 20 years at that point, was 45 years old, and through hard work and skill had become financially independent. As he watched the events of 9/11 unfold, his thoughts turned to KBW. He says that at some point he knew that if there was anything he could do to help the company, he owed it to his friends who perished to do so. He also felt that perhaps he owed it to the institution—the one that had given him the means to spend his summers playing tennis and fishing with his son.

As he watched the people he calls "the real heroes," the firefighters and EMS workers, he felt helpless like the rest of us. He decided that his contribution could be to help our firm get back on its feet so we would have the wherewithal to contribute to the family fund and take care of those left behind. His wife, he says, was initially concerned about additional terrorist attacks on the workplace, but now is quite pleased with his decision. It's not that Phil has given up his newfound lifestyle. Since his proprietary trading skills would make him an asset anywhere he went, he was another one of those plug-and-play people seamlessly blending back into the fold of the company. With an unconventional schedule, he stayed with us for six months and then departed for six months of tennis, golf, fishing, and other leisure time with his wife and family, and we're expecting him back sometime in the fall.

We were also fortunate that yet another one of our alumni was willing to come and help us out temporarily. Joe Duwan had spent 17 years with us before retiring earlier in 2001. He had been a senior vice president in the Research Department and came back as a consultant for six months to help us get our systems up and running.

During the restaffing period, we also were talking to Tom McCandless for the position of one of our senior bank analysts. Tom had been the bank analyst at CIBC Oppenheimer until the middle of 2001 when CIBC had decided to stop following the money center and large cap regionals—Tom's area. We knew him quite well, regarded him highly, and were able to get him to join us immediately. We were pleased to learn that Michael shared our impressions of Tom and was excited about having Tom join him as a senior bank analyst.

With the hiring of new staff to rebuild the company, we had to face the issue of our senior staff and board of directors. We had lost five of the nine executives who comprised our board, including my co-CEO and our chairman, Joe Berry. After much discussion, we decided to create an Office of the Chairman made up of three individuals. I assumed the title of chairman and was made the chief executive officer. We no longer felt a need to have this title shared. Andy, who was our vice chairman and director of corporate finance, was promoted to president. Tom Michaud was promoted to vice chairman and chief operating officer from executive vice president and director of equity sales.

At the same time, we elevated Michael O'Brien from president of KBW Asset Management to its CEO. Michael, the only member of our board who had been in the building and escaped, remains on the board. John Howard, one of our senior vice presidents who is the manager of our largest regional office in Hartford, joined the board and was promoted to executive vice president.

We issued a press release about these changes on October 18, approximately five weeks after the disaster devastated the company. Originally we had hoped to announce the hiring of our director of research at the same time, but delayed that announcement because of Michael Corasaniti's insistence that we formally meet with Jeff and Vincent.

Thus, on October 22, I was finally able to proudly announce the key appointments we had made in our research and trading departments. This signaled to the rest of the world that we were serious and intended to continue to be a force to contend with on Wall Street. We announced that Michael Corasaniti, Tom Mc-Candless, Vincent Daniel, Jeff Spetalnick, Joe Duwan, Phil Cuthbertson, Larry Vitale, and Al DiAntonio had all joined our team.

In addition, we promoted John Ragan to the director of equity trading position, a function that he had been filling on an interim basis since 9/11.

Once we had Michael, Larry, and Tom in place, it became apparent to us that we should use Michael as the point person going forward in terms of hiring additional analysts. Since they would work for him, we wanted to make sure he was comfortable with each of the hires. Tom, Andy, and I would also want to meet the people that Mike was leaning toward, but we left him to do the initial screening. This decision freed us from ferreting through the universe of potential candidates.

The reaction we got from our clients as we announced some of these initial hires, Mike Corasaniti, Tom McCandless, and Larry Vitale, was very positive. The fact that three individuals of their caliber had joined, or in Larry's case rejoined, KBW was a very positive message to the rest of the market. The news produced a side benefit: Other analysts who contemplating joining us had their confidence in KBW boosted by the actions of these three highly respected individuals. We intended to be here for the long run, and we intended to be first rate.

Once we had some of the research people in place, the next area that we needed to focus on was restaffing the equity trading desk. On September 11, we lost all of our market makers, that is, individuals who traded the over-the-counter stocks. We had 23 people on the equity trading desk at Tower Two, and 21 of those individuals died in the attack. As said before, the survivors were sales traders, Courtney Webber and Katie Ré. Courtney was days away from being married and had taken the day off to prepare for her wedding and Katie had the good fortune that morning to be late for work. She was on the way in when the planes hit our building. Katie still keeps her "piece-of-crap" alarm clock that did not go off that morning although she no longer uses it.

Courtney and Katie, along with Al DiAntonio, went up to our Boston office to help John Ragan and the other folks handle the trading for the firm in those early weeks. We began trading out of our Boston office, limiting the trading to listed securities. As mentioned before, we believed the Monday when the exchange opened again was going to be a very high volume day. Since we were trading out of our Boston office with limited staff, we felt that rather than make some errors in a chaotic market, we would be better served to wait a day. Consequently, we didn't begin trading again until September 18, a week after the attacks.

Our search for trading personnel was similar to the process we had used for researchers. Besides using contacts and recommendations, we examined unsolicited resumes from people who knew that our trading desk had been decimated.

One of the calls that we received in those early weeks came in the form of a fax from an acquaintance who had been at Donaldson Lufkin Jenrette (DLJ) before First Boston had acquired it. The timing was fortuitous for everyone involved. The fax arrived right around the time that we were beginning our search for the trading personnel. First Boston had announced a round of layoffs because of the slowdown in the equity business on Wall Street, especially following 9/11.

Many of the individuals on the trading side at First Boston were employees who had been part of DLJ before the merger and had worked with First Boston for roughly a year. Their jobs were either in jeopardy or they had already been laid off during the terminations in October 2001. Mark Sulam, who had been head of equity at DLJ, contacted me and told me of several former DLJ employees now at First Boston who were seriously looking for new positions. He had already suggested that they contact KBW and provided me with telephone numbers where we could reach them. Our surviving equity sales division was working out of the office space lent to us by BNP/Paribas, and we were attempting to build around that core group.

Once we were on track, we set a rather ambitious goal for ourselves. We wanted to get back into making markets for the 300 or 400 companies that we made an over-the-counter market for their stock before the end of 2001. To meet this goal, we needed to do several things in addition to hiring traders and taking care of our other human resource requirements. We needed the hardware, machinery, computers, and terminals to do the trading. We needed communication lines installed and specific software. Otherwise, we didn't stand a chance of meeting our year-end target date.

Getting the appropriate data and communication lines proved to be one of the more challenging issues. By the end of November, we managed to have an over-the-counter trading staff in place. We hired several sales traders and several over-the-counter market makers and assistants to help us in that effort.

We made our goal when we resumed market making activities in over-the-counter stocks and trading in more than 200 financial stocks on December 6, 2001. Around that time, the space allotted to us by BNP was fully wired and ready for trading and our New York people returned from Boston. Historically, we have been one of the largest market makers in the NASDAQ 100 financial stocks and are often the number one, two, or three market maker in the stocks that we trade. We have recovered our old position in the market—less than three months after our devastation.

Larry Vitale and Phil Cuthbertson were already doing some proprietary trading for us. Phil helped us interview most or all of the people that we were going to put on the trading desk. In addition to coming down from Boston a few days a week each week to interview candidates in New York, John Ragan also interviewed some prospects in Boston. In addition, Tom conducted many interviews involving the restaffing of trading personnel. KBW was the beneficiary of a dismal employment environment on Wall Street. Besides DLJ, there were other sources of talented trading personnel and talent. One of our competitors, Putnam Lovell, closed their San Francisco office in early December and we were able to hire a sales trader, Jay Hanley. He joined us as vice president of equity sales trading. In February, we launched an equity sales and trading operation from our San Francisco office with Jay heading the operation along with another new hire, Don Daniel, who joined us as an institutional equity sales trader.

Our staffing endeavors continued as we fulfilled Michael Corasaniti's requirement that we have analysts in the regions. In early January, we launched bank research in Hartford and San Francisco, hiring Adam Compton from Morgan Stanley to head up our West Coast Bank & Thrift practice along with Manuel Ramirez and Faye Elliott-Gurney from Morgan Stanley.

In Hartford, Jared Shaw, who had joined us from Friedman Billings Ramsey, began covering New England area community banks and thrifts for us. Our New York research effort was further enhanced by Thomas Monaco, who joined us after stints with Morgan Stanley, Lehman Brothers, and Bear Stearns, and Bain

Slack, who came from CIBC Oppenheimer, to work in New York covering Texas, Oklahoma, Louisiana, and Arkansas.

Spurred on by the momentum of success, we formed a new business unit in late January that focused on the brokerage of whole-loan portfolios. Incorporated as part of the investment banking division, the group, called the Loan Portfolio Sales Group (LPSG), was comprised of a seasoned team of debt-sales professionals—Lou DiPalma, Mike MacDonald, Sean McVity, and David Gavoor—with experience at two of the industry's top firms, Cohane Rafferty Securities (DiPalma and MacDonald) and Meenan, McDevitt & Company (McVity and Gavoor).

Lou and Mike headed up the origination and sales effort, while Sean and David led the firm's structuring and distribution desk. We felt that this line of business was a great complement to our existing investment-banking services and would allow us to deliver additional value-added services to our customers. In addition, the relationships with these people brought us significant new points of client contact in the banks, thrifts, finance companies, and other credit grantors in the heart of our target market. It was exactly the type of niche business that melded perfectly with our existing client base while simultaneously giving us the opportunity to expand our franchise.

Building a new staff almost from scratch was exhausting, but it also was exciting. That was the challenge facing Mike Corasaniti during his first six months on the job. He says that in the beginning all he did was recruit, recruit, and then recruit some more. His goal was to build a team with diverse backgrounds, skills, and outlooks—neither wildly bearish, nor all bullish. Similarly, he didn't want all regulators or all people from the same firm. He says he wanted disparate backgrounds to mimic what we had before—smart, hungry, hardworking people—the backbone of KBW.

In those beginning months before our new space was ready, we were faced with unique challenges. We were recruiting people who knew full well that their surroundings would not be perfect for some time, our technology was not always 100 percent, our phones would go out, and it would be months before we had what the rest of the business community would consider normal e-mail.

Despite these hurdles, there were other problems we couldn't foresee. For example, with all the construction work going on, the office temperature would fluctuate. It occasionally soared past 90 or below 50. But everyone understood that this was temporary and made the best of it.

We were lucky that we didn't have to resort to recruiting firms, although a number called and offered their services. Through our contacts and the unsolicited resumes we received, we were able to fill all the vacant positions. Of course, KBW's reputation and the state of the market greased the wheels more than a little. By the end of March, the research department had filled 22 slots and had only one remaining opening.

Those responsible for the bulk of the hiring had a tough job. They had to spend massive amounts of time reviewing resumes, interviewing candidates, and then selecting the right person. Because of our unique corporate culture and the way the firm is structured, we have to be exceedingly careful. Not only are we hiring a person to do a job, we are also getting a potential partner. At KBW, ownership is a privilege we share with all employees and is something expected of our more senior people.

The next step for us may ultimately be the most challenging. We have numerous new people and we need to integrate them into our corporate culture. Although, unlike many Wall Street firms, KBW is not a place where there are many stars, many of the people we hired come from companies that have a star mentality. This is an ego-driven business, so we could all be in for a rough ride. But I have high hopes.

We lost 67 people on September 11, 2001, and by the end of March 2002, we had invited 75 individuals to join KBW to help us rebuild the firm. Of those new hires, only one has left us. Time will be the ultimate test, but for now, I can honestly say, we've made the best start possible.

8

WHEN YOU CAN'T GO HOME AGAIN

When it came to finding a home, we had two challenges—locating immediate temporary space and then finding permanent quarters that would meet all of our requirements. Thanks to our generous friends, our temporary space needs were much easier to address than our long-term requirements.

Our first offer came in the first days after September 11 when I received a phone call from a friend, Steve Joynt, president of Fitch Rating Services. Steve volunteered that Fitch had some extra space in its downtown offices. He felt we could utilize it for some period of time. In one of my conversations with Andy in the days following 9/11, the topic of where we were going to find new offices was raised, and I mentioned Steve's offer.

Andy asked me where the proposed space was. I said I didn't know exactly but thought it was State Street downtown. There was a long pause on the other end of the phone. When I asked Andy if he was still there, I heard a gulp or a swallow and he said, "John, Tom and I have made the decision that we can't go back there."

At that point I hadn't been back in Manhattan yet and, thus, hadn't really thought about the effects of relocating downtown. After learning of Tom and Andy's resolve, I immediately agreed that the emotional stress and trauma of asking employees to go back to work near the World Trade Center location would be unacceptable. I called Steve and thanked him, explaining that we weren't able to use the space.

Next, our friends at Wachtell Lipton and BNP/Paribas had some space that was temporarily vacant that they were willing to share with us. For Wachtell, it was the second time they took us in, letting us use its conference rooms, inconveniencing its staff, with an open-handed generosity that was truly amazing.

Our accounting people worked out of space provided by KPMG Peat Marwick, our back office or trading support personnel were temporarily housed in the offices of Pershing and Company in Jersey City. Michael O'Brien arranged for our asset management people to use a conference room at Prime Brokers for the first few days. He eventually moved them into the BNP space that was, in the end, our saving grace.

Not only did BNP Paribas have temporary excess capacity on its trading floor, it was also willing to share with us until April 1, 2002. This gave us some time to find a permanent space and have it properly wired for the technology needed to run a modern state-of-the-art trading operation. The loan of suitable space for our traders also gave us some breathing room in our search for a permanent home. The bank agreed to lend us 24 desks, which initially seemed more than adequate. However, we were in a rebuilding mode and what had first seemed like more than ample room was not so at the end. Periodically, Tom would call Sue Bacon, BNP's head of premises and logistics, and wheedle a few more desks from her. I'm afraid that by

March, we were occupying 36 desks, all rigged online by our re-markable IT people.

The terrorist attacks threw a monkey wrench into our merger talks. From BNP's standpoint, the bank had to reconsider what it was getting with KBW since we had, indeed, lost a number of key people. From our vantage point, we had to rethink some alto-gether new questions about the arrangement. Was the merger still the best course of action for our employees? Would it allow us to take care of the families in the manner we wanted? Unfortunately, answers weren't easy because we were in no frame of mind to ad-equately address these questions in those first few weeks.

When we first began to look for space, the possibility of the merger influenced some of our decisions. If the merger went for-ward, it would be advantageous for our offices to be near BNP, if not in the same building. If the merger fell through, as it eventu-ally did, proximity to BNP would be totally irrelevant.

Immediately after the attack, BNP had come to the decision that as a firm it wanted to help some of the companies devas-tated by the attack on 9/11. It had made a commitment right from the start that KBW would be given top priority in the ef-fort. Roughly 48 hours after the attack, BNP's David Brunner, head of its securities unit, and Everett Schenk, head of North American Territory, called a meeting to try and figure out what the bank could do to assist.

Sue Bacon said that BNP would do whatever it could to aid us according to our needs, and its assistance was nothing less than extraordinary. Although it had not lost any of its current employ-ees, many of its 300 plus traders lost close friends and associates, and the attack was personal for many.

First, BNP's IT staff went above and beyond the call of duty to try and support everyone who needed it. Communication resources in New York City were stressed after the loss of the World Trade Center. Most people don't realize that the Trade Center was critical to communications in the city, because it housed significant equipment for routing calls, data transmissions, and the like. Thus, the BNP IT people were already under pressure as BNP itself had connectivity and system issues periodically.

BNP graciously handled a variety of mundane tasks in order to get us settled—matters that we were too frazzled to even consider. They took care of the phones, notified the building of our arrival, made sure that security gave our people IDs so they could enter the building, determined what supplies we would be need, and a myriad of other tasks.

BNP employees made signs that said, "BNP/Paribas welcomes the staff of Keefe, Bruyette & Woods," which were hung wherever our staff would be working.

Our trading operation was exiled to Boston, where we handled our listed business between the Boston and Hartford offices. We moved some of our trading personnel to those locales to help accommodate the volume. Toward the latter part of November, our trading space on BNP's eighth floor had been equipped with the needed telephone and trading lines and trading systems and we were able to start our trading in the over-the-counter market that had been suspended since 9/11.

The trading and the market making in over 300 companies was re-instituted on December 3, weeks earlier than our December 31 deadline. It was more than two months after the attack before we were at anything near full strength on the trading side of the business. We didn't feel we could afford to be out of the markets for too long before our clients, customers, and the companies whose stocks we trade would be affected and our franchise value might be affected.

Andy and Tom were in contact with a number of real estate brokers in the city as we began our search for a permanent home. With very little experience in this area, they needed some assistance—especially Andy on whom the lion's share of the burden for the search fell. Sue Bacon helped us greatly in that endeavor. Since she had previously looked at our space downtown to evaluate our IT infrastructure for the potential merger, she had a clear concept of what space we had previously occupied and was able to articulate our needs to the real estate brokers. Andy accepted her generous offer for help and the two of them toured spaces in tandem.

Since the merger was still in the discussion stages, at least initially, it was agreed that Sue would say she was a friend helping out. The brokers would ask Andy a question and he would simply look to Sue for the answer. They saw a lot of unacceptable space and a lot of less unacceptable space. Although we hadn't had the time to fully access our needs, our end objective was to assemble the full firm back in one building as soon as possible.

In the initial weeks after 9/11, the midtown real estate market was very tight. There were very few locations that we had a chance at acquiring. In the World Trade Center, we occupied about 85 thousand square feet and now we felt we needed something in the neighborhood of 50 to 70 thousand square feet, ideally on one or two floors. Such proximity helps communication between the departments, avoiding time spent in elevators or running up and down stairs.

The only space we saw in the first couple of weeks that had both the right location and enough square footage was in the Alliance Capital Building on 54th and Sixth Avenue. Although the tenant was in the process of moving out, it didn't have a trading floor or a trading desk, and would therefore need substantial renovation. Despite its great location, we couldn't be sure it could be properly configured to our needs, and so, reluctantly we decided to pass.

In the following weeks, rumors abounded of other available spaces. Bear Stearns was on the verge of moving into their new headquarters on Madison and Chase Manhattan was rumored to be taking quite a few floors in the former Bear Stearns building on Park Avenue. Intrigued, I called Mark Shapiro, vice chairman of Chase, to confirm the bank's interest in the Park Avenue space. He said they had acquired an option on the building and would probably be moving in sometime in 2002. After asking him if there was a possibility of a floor being made available for KBW, I was disappointed to learn that Chase wasn't going to take occupancy on most of the space until mid-2002 which was too long for us to wait.

Next, we turned back to BNP. In the days after 9/11, we had put our equity and fixed income teams in space offered by BNP on its trading floor on the eighth floor at 787 Seventh Avenue in the Equitable Building. We learned that there were some floors in that building that were either available or becoming so, and the Bank of New York had already acquired an option on some of space.

I placed a call to Chris (Kip) Condren, head of AXA, which owns both Equitable and the Equitable building. After confirming that Bank of New York did have an option on some space, he mentioned that he didn't know whether the Bank was going to exercise it. In response to our interest, he connected us with his real estate manager, Joe DeLuca. In the ensuing weeks, Bank of New York decided not to exercise the option on a couple of floors, and we got a look at them. By far, the space on the fourth floor of the

Equitable was the best that we had seen, especially considering our equity and fixed income salespeople, and some of our traders were already on the eighth floor.

Initially after 9/11, many of the firms downtown grabbed whatever space they could in midtown to house their employees. However. after a few weeks, some of the companies decided they didn't want to have all their people in Manhattan, perhaps fearing more attacks. They would be less crippled if their employees were based in multiple locations.

Some of the larger firms began announcing that they were looking at sites including Stamford, Connecticut; Jersey City, New Jersey; and White Plains, New York. Those announcements, plus a sharp stock market decline after the 9/11 attack, caused many firms to put their expansion plans on hold. Those companies with extra real estate realized that they might not be using that space for some time and decided to put it on the market. Therefore, between late September, when the market appeared to be very tight, and late October, a fair amount of space became available.

KBW benefited from this accordion-like real estate market. The space we'd chosen in the Equitable Building became available very quickly and we began to negotiate a lease.

The search for space and the process of signing a lease and designing the office space was certainly a lot different now than it was in 1998 and 1999 when we had moved from the 85th floor of the World Trade Center to the 88th and 89th floors. Back then, it seemed like lease negotiations and reconstruction took forever. This time around, a lot of the work we had done a few years before was applicable.

Toward the end of 1997 with our lease expiring, we realized we had outgrown our space on the 85th floor at Two World

Trade Center. We wanted to increase our space and in the process create an updated identity for ourselves. We interviewed a number of architectural firms, ultimately awarding the contract to Cetra/Ruddy in December 1997. At that point, we anticipated taking one full floor in the World Trade Center, approximately 50 thousand square feet. We had no facilities director so the architect's role on the project went beyond simply providing architectural interior design services.

Representatives from the architect's firm met with every department head and the management group to help us determine what our growth was going to be in different departments—a phase called process programming with the goal to avoid outgrowing space. From these meetings, Cetra/Ruddy created a 40- or 50-page document that was reviewed first with our CFO, adjusted to reflect his comments, and then brought for final approval to senior management. While we had some vague ideas conceptually about our future, this document spelled out both our company profile and its projections for one, three, five, and ten years in the future.

This process helped us reassess our real estate needs and led us to determine that we needed two floors. Our old management had wanted to be on as high a floor as possible with the best views. After looking at several spaces in both Towers, we took the 88th and 89th floors in Tower Two.

One of the key elements in that move was designing a state-of-the-art, sophisticated trading floor that would meet both our current needs and those we were likely to encounter in the future. The trading floor was designed to hold 90 people comfortably, giving us some room for growth.

For statutory reasons, our corporate finance department has to be segregated from the trading area. On the 85th floor, corporate finance did not have a "real presence" as the architects like to say, which means simply that it did not have a separate entrance. Therefore, a key requirement in our move to 88th and 89th floors was to create a "presence" for this group that we accomplished by placing them on a separate floor. In our old space, there was no real sense when you walked off the elevator of what our company was. Nancy Ruddy, our architect, explained how she addressed this and other issues:

> One of our really important roles was to meet with management and discuss really who they were, how they saw themselves, what their clients' perception was, and what image they wanted to portray. What I very quickly found—and we do a lot of work with Wall Street clients—was that this is a very unique company. It was first of all very flat in its hierarchy—very collegial. We found that there were people who came out of school and stayed at KBW forever. This was very different. The senior managers were a bunch of obviously very brilliant, very aggressive guys but very friendly, very loyal, and very committed to their staff. [They were also] very easy going, and a wonderful group to work with.
>
> The firm was unusual in that many of our clients have very specific ideas about what they want. The attitude of KBW was that they had interviewed a lot of professionals to do this job and [then,] made a decision. Once we were chosen, they put the responsibility in our hands and said go with it. The relationship was very interesting because we had to fit our meetings in between their deal making, mergers and acquisitions activity, and the money-making thing. But we developed what really turned out to be a terrific relationship that worked very well.
>
> Because we design from the inside out, for us an interior design project is only successful if it functions well. Aesthetics are really a by-product.

What we did was help them put departments that needed to interact adjacent to each other. We figured out which departments needed what amount of storage space, and so on. This time-consuming task paid off in a big way when we were presented with the challenge of designing new space [at the Equitable building]—quickly. [During the search for space after 9/11,] we would go with them to see a [prospective] space and then come back to our offices and work through the night to see if the space would accommodate all KBW's requirements. We did this six or seven times.

Part of the KBW corporate culture is that they bring in lunch the entire company. Food used to be all over the trading floor. [In Tower Two, 88th and 89th floors,] we created a pantry right on spot so that traders could grab their lunch while still being able to hear the activity on the trading floor.

We also created an image for them. Our sense was that even though KBW was an old firm with a lot of history, the people running it were relatively young. They had a vision of who they were and where they wanted to go and we wanted to reflect this in a setting projecting strength, power, masculinity, and at the same time, informality.

Our goal from a design standpoint was to create an ambiance that made people walking off the elevator perceive a unique company, both stable and forward looking. We used lots of wood paneling that reflects stability, age, and security. Yet the design was very forward. Very modern. Our view was that there should be high design quality and fun in the design whether you were in the pantry, a copy room, a back office area, or the highly exposed lobby and conference rooms.

Cetra/Ruddy won an award for its design of our World Trade Center space from the Society of American Registered Architects. It was announced in the summer of 2001. Part of the reason the project received the award was because of the project's high quality and its use of space. It is often easy to design quality space when the space is small. But, a hundred thousand square feet presents some unique challenges.

Nancy Ruddy and her partner and husband John Cetra came to the memorial service for the KBW employees on September 16. My wife and I were very pleased to see them. Our initial experience with them had been good and there was never any doubt about using them again for our new home. Those in the architectural community will recall seeing little about either the award or our decision to go with them again. Cetra/Ruddy, feeling it inappropriate to announce its good news about the award and new contract, pulled back all press releases about our project. Only in the spring of 2002, did they feel it appropriate to go forward with the publicity about their hire and to include information about our new home.

Nancy accompanied us to see any space we were considering. The situation that we were faced with in the fall of 2001 was very different from before. Timing and immediacy of occupancy were our first priority. Where the offices were located, what they cost, and ultimately what they looked like were secondary concerns against management's objectives to find a permanent home and reassemble all of our employees back together under one roof.

Our new trading floor presented unique issues. Many people do not realize that state-of-the-art trading floors for Wall Street firms require massive amounts of electronic and communication lines. Each desk, and there may be one hundred of them on a moderately sized floor, requires numerous hookups. The cabling—hidden behind walls, in the ceiling, and under the flooring—is extensive and requires specially trained technicians. The installation must be done before the functional items, like desks and carpeting, can be put in place.

Initially, we were very concerned about taking space that might appear luxurious because we felt it would not be appropriate given our grief. Over time, our feelings have not changed and our new space is nowhere near as opulent as our prior quarters. Despite this austerity, our real estate costs doubled—not because we were taking more space—because our new home is located in a more expensive part of town.

We were anxious to try to accommodate our employees' concerns. For example, certain people wanted to make sure they could see out a window—not demanding a window office, but simply wanting to be able to see outdoors. We also vacillated on the height issue since most of us did not wish to be on a floor that was "too high," an adjective that varied in definition. Our indecisiveness must have driven our real estate people crazy. Selecting the same architectural and design firm made things infinitely easier on that front since Nancy already knew what each of our departments would need. We, particularly Andy, were very insistent in the beginning that we did not want to be any bigger. Initially, based on the number of people we thought we would have, Nancy came up with a projection that we would need between 65 and 70 thousand square feet.

However, using the World Trade Center as a barometer, we felt that we could fit into the equivalent of one floor, or 50 thousand square feet. Nancy warned us that it would be very tight. Traditionally, we had put our people in very large offices and workstations. But now our desire to stay in close proximity, that is, on one floor forced us to bring our space standards more in line with many other comparable companies.

Nancy says that after several conversations with us our agenda was made quite clear. Though we never formalized it in writing, I agreed that she was right on target. We needed to send a message to both our own people and our customers, dispelling any rumor on Wall Street that we might merge with another firm and disappear. We wanted to project to the business community that KBW is here to stay. We cemented that sentiment when we signed a 15-year lease for the Equitable fourth floor.

With the lease in hand, we instructed our design firm to get our new space in working order as quickly as humanly possible. The floor was prebuilt. That means that most of the design work had already been done. Carpets and offices were in place. However, there was no trading floor—and we couldn't impose on BNP's good graces forever. We had to get our people off the BNP trading floor and onto our own no later than April 1.

Nancy went into action. As an outside observer, she could see us change. While initially we were not overly concerned about what our space looked like and we wanted to keep the project small, as we started to get what Nancy called our "sea legs," we began to focus more tightly. Departments that started out saying they would only need space for two or three people, began to see a brighter future, involving additional staff, and hence, additional room.

In our old Trade Center space, we had a conference room set-up with a dining room and lounge where we conducted some of our business. Initially, we did not have this arrangement in our plans, but as we reconsidered and the healing process began, we decided to add it back into the configuration—which meant another redesign of at least part of the space. Slowly, the components of our original project started to filter back. Nancy says one of my favorite lines was, "If we're going to be here for 15 years, we should think about this."

The previous tenant had furnished the space we selected in June 2001. For a variety of reasons, no staff had ever been moved in. Because we needed a trading floor, some of the space would have to be demolished and rebuilt. Initially, we anticipated redoing about 25 percent of the floor. I'm afraid that number has grown as we've started to use the space.

While we definitely do not want to replicate what we had downtown, we have asked our design team to create something that once again projects a forward-thinking firm with stability. It will be a modern looking space with a lot of wood, but much less than we had downtown.

We still faced the challenge of separating the corporate finance group from the rest of the company and also of giving the department a distinct persona. The architects have suggested we do this with a glass wall. Here's how Nancy describes it: "Because the space is so tight the wall is designed as a very beautiful, glass, architectural element, almost like a piece of artwork." Given our continued changing space requirements, the wall has been moved around on the plans. Not only will it separate the two groups, it will become the front door for the corporate finance department, the first thing visitors see when they come for a meeting with our investment bankers.

As the plans take shape, we continue to challenge the architects. Initially, seven thousand square feet was allocated for storage, in the form of four storage areas. As of the move-in date, we were down to one. Our initial plans allowed room for a gym. This too had to be scrapped as we searched for space for our ever-expanding staff.

As the staff grows, so do the technology requirements to support it. Our IT people are pretty vocal in their belief that we have not allocated enough space for our technology needs, so that's another adjustment we are going to have to make.

When it came to getting furniture for our people, availability was a key factor. We couldn't wait six months for items to be ordered and manufactured. They had to be readily available which was another limitation on the architects since they could only develop designs that could be built quickly and efficiently, without long lead times. Although they claim aesthetics had to take a back seat, I believe the architects have accomplished miracles. We had the trading desk built by the end of March 2002 and have moved most of our New York employees onto the floor.

We outgrew our wonderful new space even before we moved in, and we're already looking for additional space in the building. I believe it's a good sign, a strong signal that we are indeed recovering—at least a little—and have been successful in maintaining and growing the firm.

9

THE PAPER TRAIL: RECREATING OUR FINANCIAL PICTURE

O ne of the massive tasks we had ahead of us after September 11 was recreating our paper records—both financial and otherwise. Although much of our information had been backed up only a week earlier on our computers, we lost every scrap of paper that was on our premises. We were facing a difficult, but manageable task. Unfortunately, it was also one that had to be attacked quickly. If we were to stay in business, we needed numbers fast.

Some of our people started almost immediately getting our affairs in order. As noted earlier, Bernie Caffrey and our IT people worked out of their homes to get us up and running. Tom Michaud, John Ragan, and Bill Henningson had backed into our traders' positions using reports from Pershing. Through their efforts, we were able to limp into the market the following week.

Even our more mundane records were gone. We had lost all our employees' records and had to ask them, whether they've been with us two weeks or 20 years, to fill out new documents, contact sheets, tax records, and so on. Our life insurance documents also had to be recreated because we had kept them stored in a vault in Chase Manhattan Bank in the World Trade Center. Their loss, especially, has created some problems for the families of the victims.

We also had to rebuild the accounting function. Since we had lost our CFO, controller, and the accounts payable manager, we were hurting when it came to putting our books back together. Thankfully, we were fortunate that our remaining accounting people stepped forward and helped out including our former controller, Bob Meyer.

However, the situation was critical. During that first week, while we were using the conference rooms at Wachtell, Mitch contacted the partners from KPMG, Claudia Holtz and John Hubba, and asked to meet with them.

We were desperate, and Mitch was brutally frank in asking Claudia and John for help in rebuilding the accounting department. "Look," he told them, "We need your help and I'm not giving you the option of saying no."

You have to know Mitch to fully appreciate the situation because he's not the type of guy who orders people around. Under the circumstances, he simply did not know what else to do, and fortunately, KPMG had no intention of turning us down.

Of course, they had concerns. As anyone who has picked up a newspaper in recent months is well aware, auditor independence and impartiality are always sensitive issues. In this case, their familiarity with our books would be a big plus. Thus, on our behalf, KPMG's national practice people got in contact with the SEC, and by that weekend, the SEC had adopted a rule waiving independence concerns in conjunction with consulting for purposes of rebuilding the businesses of broker dealers who were affected by the September 11 attack.

Although, we were one of the beneficiaries of that ruling, we are very careful about building that "Chinese Wall" or firewall between the people who help us in other areas and the audit function. We want to do everything right and avoid second-guessing without even a hint that we are dealing inappropriately.

We needed accurate information and we needed it quickly. Many of the families were not only dealing with unimaginable grief, but were also attempting to make financial plans for the future. It was our goal to give them the very best information and KPMG has been very helpful as well as very careful.

KPMG assigned us one of their employees who has been working as our temporary CFO. We had lost our CFO and controller, Mike McDonnell, who was extremely well-liked by the people who worked for him. He was a hard working, no-nonsense kind of guy and the staff, who were very loyal to him, missed him tremendously. He had known where every number came from and had overseen the month-end activity including closing the books. This is a pretty important function at KBW, especially since we are employee-owned. As our business has gotten more sophisticated, the services of the accounting and finance groups are becoming more vital. We were extremely lucky in getting KPMG to assign us a person to help us through this difficult time. In addition, we had another surprise on the accounting front— Kevin Whiteside.

Like most other Americans, Kevin wanted to do something to help with the recovery efforts. He was living and working in Chicago when he decided to call Andy, who had a special relationship with Kevin's family, to express his condolences and say, "If there's anything I can do to help the company, please let me know." With his background in finance and accounting, he soon realized that he might be able to help rebuild the accounting function.

Andy asked KPMG to meet with Kevin and provide an assessment as to whether Kevin was the right person to work for us in the interim controller position. With KPMG's blessing, Kevin left Chicago and came to New York. That assignment turned into a full-time position.

Because we had backed up the system a week earlier, our record losses were not as big as they could have been. We lost our check register so we didn't even know what checks had been written in the last week, and it took months for that information to filter its way through the system.

We also had lost all invoices waiting to be paid which we handled in two ways. Once we were up and running and had figured out what invoices we thought were missing, we took a proactive approach and called our regular vendors. We didn't have to do a whole lot of explaining as it was pretty obvious what had happened.

With the rest, we just waited. Unfortunately, some companies in the rest of the country were hesitant to make collection calls to New York customers. Eventually they did call or sent second notices. However, once the invoices showed up, we then had to verify that they were legitimate. There were a few crooks out there who tried to take advantage of the situation, but when we got an invoice, it was usually pretty obvious who had ordered the goods and a few inquiries among the employees would quickly verify an invoice's legitimacy.

At one point, Mitch became uncomfortable with all the new things we were doing. He says he didn't feel he understood the way some things were being handled, and was concerned about monitoring our business. He came to the board and asked us to hire a consultant to perform a diagnostic on what was being done and what we should be doing. He wanted a list of what we needed to handle immediately and what should be considered a medium-term priority. He wanted to be able to show regulators that we were taking the right steps to identify our problems. We immediately authorized him to bring in the necessary consultants and although we ultimately expect that venture to cost close to $100,000, we believe this is money well spent in protecting both our interests and reputation.

One of the most pressing issues our accounting folks had facing them was to come up with the shareholder value as of September 30. When anyone leaves the firm, whether voluntarily or involuntarily, they are required to cash out their shares at the end of the month in which they leave. So, closing the books for that date was a top priority, but it had to be done extremely carefully and accurately for this was the cash value we would use to pay out the beneficiaries of those we lost. Initially, we felt that this had to be done no later than December 31, 2001, for tax considerations. Ultimately, when the final rulings came down from Washington, it was not necessary to meet that deadline to reduce the ultimate tax bill the families might receive.

We closed the books for September 30 right before Thanksgiving. What had normally been a two- to three-week process took almost eight weeks. Then, because of the sensitivity of the numbers, we had outside auditors review our work which added another few weeks. Although the year-end deadline turned out to be premature, it was probably beneficial, forcing us to get the work done in a timely manner.

Another good reason to move quickly was that we were facing our own fiscal year end, which coincides with the end of the calendar year. Having the auditors working for two months in our limited space didn't help, but miraculously they finished their work by the end of February. As you might imagine, the 2001 audit was a little different than normal. Since all our papers were gone, Mitch, the other people in corporate finance, and I all pitched in and helped the best we could.

At the same time as the accounting division was righting it-self, we also had to deal with the insurance issue. Our property insurer is Chubb who was extremely supportive immediately fol-lowing 9/11. Without our asking and to our surprise, we received a million dollar check right after the attack from Chubb. An ex-tremely cooperative senior person was assigned to work on our account, and we have hired KPMG's forensic team to help us pre-pare the claim with Kevin working a great deal on this matter.

It is a settlement process. We spend money; we make a claim. The insurance company doesn't want to front us too much money until we start spending it and we don't want to keep going back to them numerous times for fear of damaging our credibility. On the other hand, we don't want to be out-of-pocket for a substantial sum.

In an ironic twist of fate, we have actually benefited from the two failed IPOs and the attempted merger with BNP. In both in-stances, we had provided law firms with extensive copies of our records. We were able to get this information back which was ex-tremely useful in helping to recreate our records.

Within a few hardworking months, we have brought our ac-counting function back to full functionality and now are trying to upgrade and become more efficient. We're trying to draw on the experiences at other companies and institute the very best prac-tices. It can be an uphill battle. Most companies experience some resistance when new processes are introduced because it is inevitable that some people are more comfortable with the old familiar ways of doing things. On top of this, our staff has had more than its share of losses to deal with, but our accounting people are trying to deliver a more efficient function and quality information. Management understands the benefits of the new procedures and I'm sure our people will too when they see that they are spending more time doing work that is more interesting and less transaction based.

Looking forward, this is going to be an exciting time for both the company and the accounting function. One of the interesting dynamics we now face is the speed at which we're growing which places a lot of stress on accounting to come up with accurate and timely information. The resources of the accounting department will be stretched—but our staff is more than up to meeting the increasing demands of next year or two. They got us through what has to be the most difficult challenge a company could face—rebuilding after losing its leaders.

10

TAKING CARE OF OUR OWN: THE FAMILY FUND

Our company is very much like a family business. It's just as normal to have a conversation with someone about taking his or her kids to a baseball game as it is to discuss a business transaction. We share in our people's joys and also their sorrows. For us, the disaster was a very personal thing. As well as losing good friends, we suffered with their families and we felt that we had to help wherever we could.

Mitch Kleinman played a key role in getting us through the crisis and in helping the families. In fact, he spent every spare moment he had trying to assist them. He handled all matters that anyone didn't understand and more. Phil Cuthbertson describes Mitch as follows:

He was the only person in the firm who really understands the shareholder agreement, how the monies get paid out, in this case to the families for their ownership in the company, all the corporate governance things that are so important, particularly when people leave. He dealt with the charities and getting money to the families from the charities and accelerating claims and all these very, very difficult things that the families had to go through.

I've already told you a few of the things that our people did to help the families of those we lost. Our Hartford office spent untold hours on the phone talking to the families both helping them understand what had happened and then simply listening when needed. Many of the families availed themselves of the Hartford staff's kind hearts. Many of the surviving New York staff also spent time talking to the grieving families.

Mitch took on the role of getting information that we could pass on to the families, letting them know what they were entitled to from the company and the government. He also helped our board make decisions as to what we could do for our people.

We kept everyone on the payroll through the end of 2001, but even this was a difficult task. We learned that we were technically not paying salaries; for tax purposes, we were paying unplanned death benefits. The same classification applied to the bonuses we paid at year end. Unplanned death benefits are not called that because the deaths were unplanned (that would be too easy an explanation), but because they were not subject to a written plan under which they were paid. The reclassification was important because of tax considerations, which as you can imagine were not easy to straighten out.

We didn't know if we should withhold taxes on this amount or not and didn't get a ruling until the beginning of March. To help us understand the situation, we hired KPMG's tax group as consultants.

Although, I said we kept everyone on the payroll until the end of the year, technically, that was not true. We kept them on through the beginning of January. With all that was going on, we had informed the families but had not told our payroll service to stop the payments. We discovered this only after the payments had gone out. We could have recalled the payments since they were made electronically but decided against it. It cost the firm an extra $250,000, but we decided we would simply live with our mistake.

We were concerned about medical coverage for the families and have agreed to cover the people who were covered before 9/11 for an additional five years. In cases where an employee was married and his wife pregnant, the unborn child is covered as well. We worked with our Blue Cross/Blue Shield agent to create a separate class for the victims.

Blue Cross/Blue Shield didn't have to do this, but that they did is just another example of how many Samaritans pitched in to help wherever they could, creatively crafting solutions to aid the families of the missing and lost.

Our life insurer, Aetna, demonstrated great generosity and humanitarianism in their dealings with us. KBW's copies of our employees' beneficiary forms were lost in the disaster and Aetna didn't have any of their own. They decided they were going to pay the next of kin, even if it was later judged that they owed the money to someone else. Aetna made a second kind-hearted decision regarding death benefits. Like most companies, we have a travel policy that provides for additional life insurance of $100,000 per employee should that employee be traveling at the time of death. Aetna paid this even though it was not required.

We decided during the first week, that it would be a good idea to update the families on the direction things were taking, so we arranged a conference call with them. We wanted to share the information we had and the issues Mitch had uncovered. I spoke, along with Andy and Mitch, on the financial and business matters relating to the deaths of our employees. We received a mixed reaction from those in attendance. Some thought what we had to say seemed clinical and cold, but many others appreciated the information. As Mitch said afterwards, "it was one of the first times I realized that you could do the very best you could and still be criticized—and you just have to accept that." It was also our first inkling that no matter what we did, a few of the families would not be able to get past their loss and realize that we were there to help.

We realized during the first few days that some of the families wanted to get together and might need a place to meet with others in the same situation. So, we took a suite at the Plaza, where people could gather. We thought some families might show up the day after we announced this decision. But, that very day we got a call from the hotel saying that people were arriving. We always made it a point to have at least two or three KBW people there to sit with them, as well as a psychiatrist for grief counseling. While we were always able to ensure the presence of our people, counting on a psychiatrist was not as simple as it sounds.

We have a contract with Harris Rothenberg, a human resource or employee assistance company who provides companies with assistance regarding issues like alcohol or drug abuse. We had formalized our arrangement with them in mid-2001. As you might imagine, 9/11 overwhelmed them. Despite trying their best to meet everyone's needs, they simply could not keep up with the demand that followed the attacks—demand that came not only from companies in the World Trade Center but firms all around the city. Therefore, while we attempted to have a grief counselor in the suite at all times, this was not always the case.

One of the big issues on the minds of the families was the Federal Victims' Compensation Fund. Mitch got involved in that process early on, traveling to Washington with representatives from some of the other affected firms for a meeting in October. He's met with the Fund manager several times and I went along for one of those meetings. It was a very sensitive situation, which made it difficult to resolve the issues to everyone's satisfaction.

Sitting home that first week of 9/11 and watching the television, I noticed there were many announcements about the different relief funds being set up for the victims' families and for the firemen and policemen and other service workers who had been killed in the attack. In a telephone call with Andy one afternoon during that first week, he told me about our Shepherd program and how our executives hoped it would help families sort through their confusion and loss.

Few people, including myself, would have all the knowledge and resources necessary to deal with the insurance companies, the Federal Victims' Compensation Fund, the conflicting information emanating from the press and Washington, and everything else, like the new tax issues. The list was endless. It was all new to us. We had a number of families who were going to need assistance in dealing with financial planning, something their spouses had handled in the past. However, we did have a few advantages. For starters, we had Mitch Kleinman. The Shepherd program has proved invaluable; we hope it will lead to lifelong relationships between the Shepherd and the family.

In another telephone call with Andy, I suggested that one of the things we could offer the families was KBW's intent to establish a family fund. The monies raised for the fund would provide financial assistance to families in the days and months and years ahead. At Andy's direction, we accepted an offer made to us by North Fork Bank.

North Fork Bank is based in Melville, Long Island, and has strong relationships with many of the Wall Street firms. One of North Fork's executives had extended the offer that they would be happy to do anything that they could do to help us. We asked them to establish an account for those who wished to make a donation to the families of those missing and lost. This account evolved into the KBW Family Fund, which reached almost $10 million by the close of February 2002. The donations have been used to alleviate the expenses the 30 affected families will have in the months and years ahead. Another portion of the fund will be used to ensure that the children who lost a parent on 9/11 will have the necessary finances to pay for college. It is our intent to continue to raise money for the KBW Family Fund in the years ahead to ease the financial burden of these families as much as we can.

The clients and customers of KBW as well as some of our competitors have been extraordinarily generous in their contributions to the fund. Jefferies & Company, a Wall Street firm, announced to its clients that it intended to donate all of their commissions from trading on October 11, 2001, to the different funds that had been set up to help the families of those who perished on 9/11. That trading day for Jefferies was extraordinarily successful and resulted in a very large donation to our Family Fund. Not only did the firm donate its commissions from that day, in addition, many of its employees donated that day's salary.

Following Jefferies' lead, we decided to have our own trading day, in fact, two trading days, to duplicate what Jefferies had done. We scheduled them on October 29 and 30, 2001. Once again our clients and customers were extraordinarily generous in terms of the amount of business they directed to us on those days. We earned extraordinary commissions in this period, resulting in gross commissions of approximately $4.7 million dollars—an all-time record for KBW. This entire amount was contributed to the Family Fund.

Not only did our clients send commissions, they wrote checks personally as well. For example, Robert Arnold from Delaware Management in Philadelphia, walked into the office one day and delivered several thousand dollars of personal checks collected from the employees of his firm. Even more touching, Dave Bugajski not only collected contributions from his colleagues but gave us a lasting tribute. When his son was born shortly after 9/11, he named him Andrew Keefe Bugajski. These are just a few examples of the many kindnesses shown to KBW.

We welcome additional contributions to the fund. Checks made out to the KBW Family Fund can be mailed to: KBW Family Fund, North Fork Bank, 275 Broad Hallow Road, Melville, NY 11747, Acct. #4844.

Andy Granger, one of the traders in our Hartford office, said that these were two of the busiest days of his life. He points out that many people think the financial services industry is very cold and calculating, but on those two days, the public had a chance to see a different side of the financial community. Our staff in Boston worked overtime just to accept and transact all the business we were offered. Making money became a tertiary concern to helping our company and the families heal.

Contributions came from numerous places. Pequot Capital, the hedge fund, sent a huge check. One of our competitors showed up unannounced with an envelope. It contained a corporate contribution along with personal checks from a dozen individuals who worked at the firm. In those first few weeks, Andy got a similar gift from another Wall Street firm. Still in a daze at that point, he simply gave the envelope to his assistant. A few days later it occurred to him that he hadn't even looked to see how much it was for, he was so touched by the gesture. To his amazement, the envelope contained a $200,000 contribution.

When the market first opened on September 17, there were many whose hearts were just not ready to go back to the old ways. One such person was Michael Stead, the chief investment officer of SIFE Trust Fund, a mutual fund that specializes in financial stocks. He devoted a large portion of his time raising money for the Family Fund. "Trading doesn't matter on days like this," he said, "there are more important matters to attend to." This outpouring of support has been just amazing.

Initially it was our intention in 2002 and the years ahead to donate the commissions from each September 11 to the KBW Family Fund. We hope that those trading days are as successful as the ones we had in 2001. We still intend to designate a day for this purpose yearly, although we are internally debating whether 9/11 is the best choice. Our reasoning is that some other companies have set up similar funds—intending to donate proceeds from activity on future 9/11s. Do we all want to compete for the same money? After all, how much trading can the corporate world do in one day?

There is another consideration. There is a petition to make September 11 a national holiday. Should that happen, we'd have no trading income that day. Whether it is 9/11 or a different date, once we reach a decision, we will let the world know and look forward to the spirit of generosity our clients have continued to display.

While our efforts and the contributions to the Fund from both our friends and strangers have been impressive, we continue to look for ways to raise additional monies. All donations will be gratefully accepted and are 100 percent tax deductible. I was recently quoted in the *Wall Street Journal* as saying, "I felt like I was standing in a soup line. We were grateful for what we got, but we didn't want to be there."

Earlier, I alluded to the fact that not all of the families are pleased by what KBW has done. A few have taken exception to our focus on supporting those families with a particular financial need. Others blame us for not forcing their spouse, sibling, or child out of the building that morning. Believe me, I wish someone had dragged those who remained out. But no one can second-guess their decisions for staying.

I hope you can see by the sampling of stories I've shared that we tried and continue to strive to help the families in any way possible. Fortunately, we have been supported in this effort by our remaining staff, our customers and friends, strangers, and even some of our competitors. Though I have mentioned some by name, there are many others who have stepped forward to help us. I thank them all.

We cannot bring back the people we lost. No amount of money can replace them or lessen the grief and suffering of the survivors. I am especially concerned about the children who lost a parent. The focus of the KBW Family Fund is, to use Tom's apt description, "support not restitution." We don't want any child to go without the basics. We can't bring their parent back. We can only try as best we can to provide some assistance to alleviate the financial problems that sometimes accompany parental loss.

A NEW HOME,
A NEW BEGINNING

We knew we'd have to be out of our temporary office space by April 1, 2002. Realizing this deadline, but also understanding how easily construction can be delayed, our architect suggested that we tell everyone that our official move date was a week earlier. This was discussed in many of our management meetings and I thought we all understood the difference between the announced move date and the real move date. What I failed to factor in was Tom Michaud's crushing workload. He was so busy trying to rebuild the trading staff that he rarely attended an entire meeting—and completely missed the fact that we had an extra week leeway. So, the trading group operated under the assumption that they would be moving on March 25.

As it happened, this misunderstanding worked in our favor. In any move, especially that of a trading floor, most of the work is done on the weekend. Easter came early in 2002 and if we had kept the original move date, we would have had to ask our staff to work through Easter weekend. Instead, the weekend work was done the prior week and our people officially moved on March 25—the same day the memorial service was held for Harry Keefe at St. Patrick's Cathedral.

"The good news is we're ahead of plan," Tom Michaud explained to the press. "The bad news is we never had a plan." That about summarizes it. We have 60 desks on the trading floor taking up approximately 6,100 square feet. The area can be expanded so we'll have some flexibility as we grow.

While at one point, the idea of grouping everyone in New York held a certain attraction, it no longer does. We now have 130 people in our New York location compared with the 171 we had before the attack. Our Hartford group moved into much larger quarters and there's some room for growth there—which is probably very good given the fact that we are already somewhat cramped in our new New York office.

We've hired 75 new people and only one has left thus far. We've been very careful in recruiting, cognizant not only of people's skill sets but also of their personalities and how they will fit in. I think we've done a good job. New faces seem odd to us because we've had very little turnover in the past. KBW is as close to a family-run firm as you can get without actually being biologically related.

When the head of sales trading recruits people, he tells them that in the nine years he's been doing this not one market maker has left. Three sales traders have departed; two of them retiring and the third returning, which equals a net turnover of zero in nine years. That certainly says something about the company.

Our people not only lost 67 coworkers on 9/11, many of them lost friends. They have to deal with that grief. Many people spent hours on the telephone listening to the grief of the victims' families, unable to do anything but listen. For some, the heartbreak of that grief has begun to fade; others still live with it.

Our people had another agonizing decision to make in the weeks following 9/11. Which memorial service were they going to attend? With 67 services planned over the span of perhaps two months, it was inevitable that there would be conflicts. I could not attend the service of Joe Berry Sr., my co-CEO. It was scheduled at the same time as my son's. The memorial services were not easy to witness nor did they become any easier after attending a few; if anything, the situation became even more difficult. Six months later, some people still could not speak about their experiences without crying.

Perhaps the best explanation of how we are doing comes from Tom Michaud. He says about the families, "Everyone is devastated, but most are coping, especially those with children. We are truly strengthened by seeing how they picked up and are moving forward." I couldn't have said it better myself.

The challenge of rebuilding our company and supporting the KBW Family Fund has revitalized many of our people, including myself. As tragic as the past year has been, KBW is determined and optimistic about its future. Ours is a place where meritocracy is valued.

We've put together a fantastic team and the challenge we face now is executing our strategy. We're positive we can do it.

Our employees want to honor those lost. Andrew Cullen is a good example of this sentiment. Andrew, one of the few people on the fixed income side who escaped that day, decided he wanted to assume the position his good friend and fellow Scotsman, Derek Sword, had held. Derek had built a thriving international business for KBW and as Andrew describes it, "Tom Michaud gave me the opportunity to see if I could carry it on."

Andy believes that that if "we can be as successful as KBW was in past, our colleagues will be proud of us." I concur.

AFTERWORD:
FATHERS AND SONS

I wasn't the only father whose child worked at the firm. My co-CEO, Joe Berry Sr.'s son, Joe Berry Jr. was also employed at the firm. Joe had joined us permanently six years ago, straight out of college. Before that, on summer vacations during college, he had interned for us every year except one when he worked at Merrill Lynch. When he graduated, Joe had two job offers, one from Merrill Lynch and the other from KBW.

After talking to several of our younger employees, Joe Jr. made his decision. The persuasive argument did not come from his father but rather from one of his young associates who asked him, "Why would you want to work there when you could be here? At Merrill you would just be one of thousands struggling to get ahead against great odds, while here, you'd get to really participate." That clinched it for Joe Jr. and he joined the firm.

Joe Jr. has said that many people asked him if it was difficult to work at a company where his father was co-CEO. He responded, "Absolutely not. I was proud to work for him, happy to come to work and see him every day; watch him do what he did. I have a fairly thick skin so I never minded when people said that

I was taking advantage of a nepotistic situation. When an opportunity presents itself, you take advantage of it." At the end of 2001, we promoted Joe Jr. to vice president, a spot he earned through hard work.

Being the son of a high-ranking executive at any company can be difficult, but Joe Jr. successfully navigated those waters. When my son Christopher found himself in the same situation, he turned to Joe for guidance. Christopher also began as an intern and wasn't sure if he would stay on permanently. Frankly, I was concerned, that he might encounter some resentment from other employees. I wasn't sure that KBW would be the best place for him.

However, Frank Doyle on the trading desk liked Christopher's work and offered him a permanent spot. That's when Chrisopher turned to Joe for advice. He confided that he wasn't sure I wanted him here. He thought I'd prefer him to find his own way—and I did. But he had earned his place at KBW and had proven that when Frank offered him the job.

Joe Jr. asked Chris if he liked working at KBW and when Chris responded affirmatively, Joe Jr. replied, "Don't tell your dad I'm telling you this but this is a great place for a young person to get experience, to learn and get responsibilities that you are just not going to get at a large firm. So, if you like it and Frank wants you to stay, then stay. Tell your Dad you are taking it. He's not going to tell you not to."

Joe Jr. confided that it wasn't really a problem being the boss' son, especially if you worked in a completely different department than your father, which both Joe Jr. and Chris ultimately did. As a result, Christopher became a full-time employee of the company.

I was not concerned about showing favoritism toward my son at work; that just wasn't going to happen. Still I was afraid that Chris, like Joe Jr., would have to contend with other employees assuming that because he was the boss' son he knew all the firm's inner secrets. Nothing could be further from the truth. Joe Sr. went out of his way to make sure his son was aware of nothing before the rest of the employees knew. Joe Jr. says his father would even use subterfuge at times to ensure the confidentiality of certain information.

That was true right up until the end. At the time of the attack, we were having talks with BNP about a possible merger. Only a few top executives knew about it and Joe's father was one of them. Early on, he was involved in these negotiations and was about to go to Paris for a meeting with BNP to discuss some of the issues involved. Joe Jr. happened to be home the weekend before 9/11 and saw his father's airline tickets on the dining room table. Like many of our employees, he had heard the rumors of our talks. "What's this for?" he asked.

"Nothing special," his dad replied, "just a business meeting."

That weekend was the last Joe Berry's family would spend together. Joe Jr. and his father talked again on Monday night trying to decide where to take his mother for her birthday dinner the next day. They had decided on Nino's Positano.

Joe Jr. was just putting on his shirt getting ready for work, when the first Tower was hit. His roommate heard it on the news and called in to him, "Do you work in the Tower with the point or the other one?"—the antenna question again.

Joe Jr. quickly ascertained that it was not the KBW building that had been attacked and continued getting dressed. His immediate reaction was that this was nothing serious, but he would probably end up having the day off. He tried to make some calls but the telephones were not working. As he prepared to leave, the second building was hit. Like most other people, he now realized that there was much more involved than a pilot error in a small plane.

He immediately tore off his tie and dress shirt, grabbed a tee shirt and his bike, and headed downtown. Before leaving, he asked his roommate to remain in the apartment in case, by some miracle, the telephones started working again. He knew if he could get close enough to see the building, he would be able to determine if the plane had hit above or below where the KBW offices were located. This was crucial information that he hoped to be able to share with his mother who he knew would be frantic when she learned what had happened.

Joe Jr. was able to get downtown because he was on a bike. As he stood looking at the South Tower, an announcement came over a police bullhorn. "Everyone run, there's another plane."

This is not the type of announcement that is usually made to a crowd but the police became desperate when they heard the sounds that turned out to be army planes patrolling the area. The crowd, including Joe, dispersed. He biked through several streets ending up close to our building—just in time to see it fall.

Joe Jr. is a pretty realistic guy and he knew at that point that if his father were still in the building, he was gone. When he finally connected with the rest of his family that day and learned that his brother Todd, who worked on the floor of the New York Stock Exchange, had been on the phone with his dad from almost the moment the first plane hit until the second plane flew into the Tower, he abandoned all hope and tried to prepare for the inevitable.

Instead of returning to his apartment, he headed for his parents' home in New Jersey, not wanting his mother to be alone at this horrible time, on a day that was also her birthday.

Joe Jr. didn't return to work on September 12 although he praises those who did work tirelessly in the days following to rebuild the firm. The typical professional lost that day had been with the firm an average of 14 years. Whole departments were destroyed. However, those that remained pitched in almost immediately to begin both the task of rebuilding and equally as important, the effort to assist the families of those who were gone.

Joe Jr. lost so much that day. Not only did his father perish but many friends and associates died with him. For the past few years, Joe Jr. had done some of the college recruiting for the firm and was instrumental in hiring many of the young people who died that day. He had recruited five people from college that spring, most of them starting sometime during the summer. All but one was lost on 9/11.

Asked about regrets for his dad, Joe Jr. can focus on only one area. He feels his father did not get to enjoy the fruits of his labor. He had been getting up at 5:30 A.M. and leaving the house 15 minutes later to make that morning meeting for almost 30 years. Other than his clothes, he was not a man who made much of material possessions, owning no boat or fancy car. However, he and his wife had recently built a summer home in Amagansett, New York, on eastern Long Island. Joe Sr. had hoped to start spending some time there, not necessarily retiring but perhaps not putting in the long grueling hours he had endured for so many years.

The fact that his father didn't get to enjoy all he had worked for drives Joe Jr. even harder to make sure KBW survives and thrives.

Joe considers himself fortunate. Despite the tragic loss of his father, he feels incredibly lucky that he and his brother and sister, all in their twenties, had the time to get to know their father and the kind of man he was. He says he will use the lessons he learned from Joe Sr. all his life. He feels bad that the younger children of the victims of the tragedy will never get to know their fathers the way he knew his.

When asked to share a business story about his father, Joe Jr. chose one he heard second hand. Several weeks after 9/11, his mother got a call at 2 A.M. from a woman in Singapore. She told the family that she used to work for a company that rented space on the same floor in the World Trade Center as KBW in the mid-1980s. She arrived at work at the same time as Joe Sr. and they often rode the elevator together. One day he noticed she looked a little upset and he asked her if everything was okay. She confided that her boyfriend had recently asked her to marry him and she was worried because he was domineering and she feared losing her independence. She didn't know what to do.

The guidance she received from Joe Sr. was all she needed to make her answer a yes. "I can speak to you from experience," he told her, "marriage is a wonderful thing. You have nothing to fear. If you love the person, then do it." She followed his advice and moved to Singapore with her new husband. She called to let the family know that the advice had changed her life, that she was happy and very grateful for it. She concluded by sharing how very special she thought Joe Berry Sr. was.

KBW is in the blood of the Berry family. It is important to them that the firm be rebuilt and they intend to help as much as they can. Joe Jr.'s cousin Paul will be joining the firm in August 2002, in the equity sales department—the same place his uncle started almost 30 years earlier. Joe's brother Todd will leave the

New York Stock Exchange to join the KBW trading desk. For Joe Jr., it is important to him that the firm be rebuilt. His father spent almost 30 years at KBW and was one of the first people hired as the company started to take off. His father was his friend and mentor and he admired him in more ways than his father probably knew. He wants to do whatever he can to help bring the firm back to where Joe Sr. envisioned it would be.

In memoriam

KBW had its offices on the 85th floor in the World Trade Center in 1993. Most of its employees were in the building when the bomb exploded in the garage. Although there were some close calls (several employees were stranded in an elevator for hours), all made it out safely. Richard Stillinger, a KBW employee, wrote the following poem at the end of that year reflecting on the firm's experiences:

The Year of the Bomb

We somehow knew we weren't quite safe,
When Crowley left the firm;
Then some of us began to chafe,
To fidget, fret and squirm.

'Twas bad enough when Sally left,
And then recessive Gene;
So we felt even more bereft
When Don Z. fled the scene.

There loomed a formless, nameless threat
of bad luck, danger, loss;
By premonitions sore beset,
We questioned The Big Boss:

What's gonna happen Mr. Lott?
Why are we so afraid?
"There, there, he soothed us on the spot;
This firm has got it made!"

"With merger fees and other gains,
We'll have a banner year;
Just don't leave any coffee stains,
Speak up, so we can hear,"

"And, you will have your just reward,
With bonuses galore;
You ain't seen nothin' yet," he roared:
"Forget what went before!"

Thus reassured, we came back to work
That February day,
Not dreaming that Fate's latest quirk
Would soon hold us at bay.

So Steverino and Planage
The elevator rode;
But far below, in that garage,
Preparing to explode,

The newest megabomb in town
Was getting set to blow
While Steve and Bobby headed down
With—yes—Vice Chairman Joe.

Then suddenly the building shook,
Unsettled by the blast;
And here above, a queasy look
Spread through the office fast.

Uneasy rested Roz's head;
Her face took on a pall,

"Don't worry, Roz," I blithely, said,
"Construction work, that's all!"

But once again a Research guess
Turned out to miss the mark;
Construction no, a bombing yes, -
And, hanging in the dark,

Cut off from all the world around,
Were Bobby, Joe and Steve;
They longed to get back on the ground,
But found it hard to leave.

The rest of us, cut off as well,
At least were less in pain;
Not subject to a private hell
Like Berry, Walsh and Plane,

Who nonetheless, as salesmen apt,
Kept pushing favorite stocks
To client Wooden, also trapped
In that suspended box;

"I'll buy, I'll buy," he shouted loud,
"Just get me outa here!"
I can't resist this wild Keefe crowd:
They're playing on my fear!"

The hours dragged, but finally
The wall was broken through;
Our elevated friends were free
To leave that frantic zoo,

While we above could take our ease;
A little smoke—no flame;
We lolled about with wine and cheese
Until the firemen came.

But then we mustered all the troops:
    A full house, on the whole;
McDermott checked the various groups
    And quickly called the roll,

"Who's missing here? Speak up!" said he;
    "Well, Jim, Dick's on the phone;"
McDermott rubbed his hands with glee:
    "Let's just let him here alone!"

"He hasn't finished that report;
    Until he gets it done,
We'll strand him here ? hey, what great sport!
    The ultimate in fun!"

Because of that outrageous pact,
    Old Dick remained behind;
I've been here ever since, in fact,
    Just sticking to the grind.

Well anyway, we all survived;
    We've had that banner year;
And now, with spirits full revived,
    We welcome Christmas cheer;

We look beyond to '94
    Without a sense of dread;
The bombing's past, we know the score,
    And see clear skies ahead.

REMEMBRANCES

Marie Abad

Marie Abad, 49, was senior vice president in the fixed income department of KBW. For 23 years, Marie treated KBW employees like they were family. They, in turn, referred to her as "The Mayor."

Once in a while you meet a person who will make a profound impact on your life, someone unique in every way and someone very special. Not a Mother Theresa, a Lady Diana, or a Jackie Kennedy but someone much closer to our ranks and just as valuable. Someone you are proud and happy to know and have as a friend. Such a person was Marie.

She didn't pick her friends; they picked her. If there is one word that could describe Marie if would be "life." That is exactly what she represented, life itself. It wasn't so much that she preached it; she wasn't the type to preach. It was something she did every day, day after day. It's been said Marie never had a "bad hair" day. She always saw the cup as half full not half empty. On a dreary day, it wasn't the cloud she would notice but rather the little ray of sunshine that was trying to permeate through the clouds. Marie would let you know when it did because that is what she was about.

The one thing that you couldn't miss about Marie was her smile, which was always present. It didn't matter what time of day it was, how busy it was, or what tasks lay ahead, it was always there. She loved KBW, her job, and everyone with whom she worked. This was her other "family." The only time she was happier was when she was with her husband Rudy, her parents Jimmy and Jennie, and her brother and sister-in-law Dee and Madeline. That was when you saw her smile get even bigger.

You couldn't say enough about Marie. She was as loving and lovable as anyone you will ever meet. Her loss cannot be described. Anyone who knew her knows exactly how this loss feels. You can never replace someone as dear as her. A "Marie" comes along only once in a lifetime.

Joao Aguiar Jr.

Joao Aguiar Jr. (JJ) led the trading effort at KBW Asset Management since August 1999. His responsibilities included developing trading relationships with other broker-dealers, executing equity and fixed income trades for KBW AM's various funds and separate accounts, settling trades with our prime brokers, and keeping track of fund positions. JJ previously worked at the Fuji Bank, Ltd managing and trading the bank's interest rate risk in their money markets group.

JJ received his BBA in finance from George Washington University and had recently completed his Chartered Financial Analyst (CFA) designation after several years of hard work and persistence. He was very proud of his accomplishments.

He was fun-loving and intense at the same time. He loved going to his uncle's beach house and being with his friends. His parents live in Portugal and he had just recently found the love of his life. JJ could pick up your spirits with his humor and zest for life. We will miss him tremendously.

David S. Berry

David S. Berry was executive vice president and director of equity research at KBW and a member of the board of directors since 1999. David's coverage of the banking industry focused on the large money-center banks and the credit card companies. He had joined the firm in 1986 and rose through the ranks of the research department, eventually becoming its head in 1995. He was often quoted in the *Wall Street Journal* and other financial press and was respected by his peers throughout the industry.

David was known within the firm and outside it for his thorough scholarly research. He was a bright star in a bright constellation. He graduated from Yale University in 1980 and then studied at the London School of Economics. He always struck us as being more of a New Yorker or Londoner than someone who was born in Oklahoma.

David and his wife, Paula, lived in Brooklyn with his three wonderful sons: Niel, Reed, and Alexander. He spoke with his wife, mother, and father the morning of 9/11 after the first plane hit Tower One. We'll miss him always.

Joseph John Berry

Joseph John Berry was born on January 28, 1946, in Queens, New York. He attended the Arch Bishop Molloy High School and graduated from Queen's College in 1969 with a BA in Economics. After graduation, he taught mathematics at the Christ the King High School in Queens, New York, while simultaneously attending graduate school at St. John's University. He graduated from St. John's University in 1971 with a Masters in Business Administration.

Joe began his career with Keefe, Bruyette & Woods, Inc. in 1972 as vice president of institutional equity sales. He then rose to senior vice president, executive vice president, president and chief operating officer, and finally co-chief executive officer and chairman of the firm. In 1985, he began assisting Charles Lott in managing the KBW profit sharing plan. In this latter stage of his career, Joe's responsibilities included managing the profit sharing plan, managing the sales/trading and asset management business of KBW and helping to draft and manage the strategic direction of the firm.

Joe had a zeal for investing and was entirely competent in that endeavor. Over his many years managing institutional client accounts, he developed strong personal relationships with his clients. Many trusted inherently in his bank stock picks. Joe did not particularly enjoy the limelight. In addition, he was never entirely comfortable speaking in front of large crowds and preferred to deflect credit rather than take it. He grew into his successively senior roles quickly and developed a knack for leading through consensus.

Despite his business successes, many will remember him more for his impeccable taste in clothes, the perfect knot in his ties, his easy smile, and his likeable demeanor. Joe was as comfortable and happy "chatting" with strangers in the elevator as he was talking to with the CEO of the largest banks in the country.

Joe is survived by his children, Joseph Jr., Todd, and Kim Berry, as well as his wife Evelyn.

Jeffery D. Bittner

Jeffery D. Bittner, 27, was an associate in the research department at KBW since joining the firm in 1997. Jeff's coverage focused on nationwide specialty finance companies and banks and thrifts located in the Southeast and the Midwest. Jeff was recognized for having a keen and adaptable talent as a research analyst, as demonstrated by his ability to assess a wide variety of challenging business models.

Jeff was introduced to KBW by his fellow KBW research analyst and native of Wethersfield, Connecticut, David Winton. He attended and graduated from Middlebury College before moving to New York City. There, he enjoyed the company of his roommates and many friends. In the last weeks before the attack, he had joined a mentoring program that made him a big brother to New York City school children.

Jeff leaves an older brother, father, and twin sisters. He always will be remembered by his fellow KBW employees for his constant good cheer, sense of humor, and powerful mind.

Krystine Bordenabe

Krystine Bordenabe, 33, started with KBW in 1999 as a fixed income assistant. She was a very knowledgeable person when it came to fixed income transactions. Krystine's bright personality kept all of our customers happy.

Krystine was the type of person that everyone enjoyed having around, she was a tell-it-like-it-is kind of person, no nonsense; "You don't like it, too bad" was her favorite line. To hear her say it made you laugh. She was a lot of fun and we miss her.

At her time of hire, Krystine was a proud single mom of 11-year-old Andrew Godsil. She married Freddie Bordenabe on August 12, 2000. Shortly after her wedding, she and her husband purchased their new home and found out that she was pregnant. Krystine felt that all her hard work and dedication were finally paying off. She was ecstatic with her new life as Mrs. Bordenabe, her new home, and the anticipation of having a brand new baby. Her husband Freddie treated her son Andrew as if here were his own. Krystine had no more worries; she had a great job here at KBW, a wonderful husband, a terrific son, and a daughter on the way. Krystine was a wonderful friend, a true angel, and she will always be in our hearts.

Nick Brandemarti

At 21 years of age and on his way to the top of the world, Nick Brandemarti started his professional journey in July 2001 as a research analyst for KBW. The move to the Manhattan firm seemed natural for Nick after graduating from Fordham University with a BS degree in Finance.

While at Fordham, Nick competed for the Rams football team. The ultimate teammate on and off the field, Nick was presented the Bill Tierney Spirit Award for his dedication to the program. With a glimpse of his smile and determined demeanor, one knew that he was destined for greatness. A single encounter with Nick would show that his intelligence and intensity were only matched by his slapstick sense of humor.

A native of West Deptford, New Jersey, Nick was known for his kindness to others and gregarious personality. No matter the situation, Nick always had the ability to elevate the spirits of those around him. Even more impressive was his zest for life. He often read motivational books and enjoyed hiking, scuba diving, and golf.

However, Nick's greatest passion was his family. He cherished going to Sunday Mass with his mother Nancy and curling up on a couch to view a movie with his sister Nicole. He treasured the time he spent listening to his father Nick's wisdom and endless collection of jokes. Who could forget the way Nick beamed when watching his brother Jason chase opposing quarterbacks for Lycoming College Warriors? There are countless more memories of Nick shared by his family and friends. It is these memories that keep Nick's essence alive in everyone who knew him.

David O. Campbell

David O. Campbell or DOC (as he was affectionately called), 51, was a senior vice president in equity sales at KBW. He became an intricate part of KBW's New York office after serving five years of hard time at KBW's Hartford office. This was his second career as he began working 13 years earlier at the accounting firm of Deloitte, Haskins & Sells.

Not only was DOC dedicated to his job at KBW, he also loved what he did. He was truly concerned about the people with whom he dealt. His clients knew DOC as the most genuine person they ever met. And he always maintained the highest level of integrity.

DOC had many friends and he never passed up and opportunity to have a good time. Particularly close to him were his Rutgers DKE frat brothers and his Deloitte golfing buddies. Furthermore, he was held in high esteem at KBW for his constant upbeat, fun-loving spirit.

Beyond this, Dave was devoted to his wife Cindy and their two sons Chip and Tim. Sunday nights were memorable nights because he spent it with family and a sprinkle of close friends. He spent innumerable hours supporting his sons' hockey, lacrosse, and golf careers. DOC's spirit was ever present at the Meadowlands Arena in March when his sons realized their father's dream for them by winning the New Jersey State Hockey Championship victory for Delbarton.

Kevin N. Colbert

Kevin N. Colbert, 24, was with KBW for less than a year, but as soon as you spoke with him you felt as if you had known him for a lifetime. Kevin was hired in operations to handle cash and bond transactions. After working with Kevin, you quickly learned that he was a jack of all trades.

Kevin's bright smile and personality made our operations group feel like a family. He was the big little brother we all loved. At only 24 years of age, Kevin had accomplished more than most people. Shortly after attending Hofstra University, he moved into an apartment near Battery Park with his girlfriend. He played every sport there was and was very family oriented. On a daily basis, Kevin would have a new story about his brothers or his mom. Kevin was an amazing person who was loved by all and will be greatly missed. In honor of Kevin, there is now a scholarship fund at Hofstra University. As Kevin would say, "Take care, comb your hair."

Donald Delapenha

Donald Delapenha was a senior vice president and the head corporate bond trader for the fixed income sales and trading division of KBW. Don joined the firm as a bond trader in 1993. He was known as the Crusher at the trading desk, a nickname he earned as a football player in college mainly because he was such a powerfully built man. However, his physical presence did not overshadow his personable salt-of-the-earth demeanor and quick sense of humor. Those who met Don recognized early on that he was a gentleman in the truest sense. He respected people and had the trust of those with whom he worked.

Even though he was a senior bond trader, Don remained humble and tried to make everyone feel that they were part of a successful team. He was the last to boast and the first to lend a helping hand. Don had a keen interest in current events and politics. He was a true patriot with conservative ethics. Don kept a small American flag on his desk next to the many pictures of his family. He enjoyed vacations with his family and being in the outdoors. Whether on a golf course or raking leaves in his back yard, he never missed an opportunity to wear long shorts and a sweatshirt—even on a cold November day.

Don was born and raised in New Jersey. He graduated from Baldwin-Wallace College in Cleveland in 1985 and was a member of the Lambda Chi Alpha Fraternity. He lived in Allendale, New Jersey, with his wife Lorraine and their three children—daughters Samantha and Madison, and son Robert.

While Don will be remembered for his integrity and professionalism at work, most of all he will be remembered as a man who truly cherished his family life.

Debra Ann DiMartino

Debra Ann DiMartino, 36, was the vice president of the equity trading department, and was somebody to everyone—mother, wife, daughter, friend, and confidant. Debbie was a KBW veteran, who joined the firm 16 years ago. She began her career as an operations specialist and decided she wanted to work on the trading desk. After learning all the functions there were to know in the back office, she was given an opportunity to move onto the Equity Trading Desk and jumped at it. As the only female of the department at that time, the environment was a challenge but Debbie was up to it. After backing up market makers for a period of time, Debbie eventually began to trade the thrift conversions herself. As much as she loved the risk of the trading desk, she also loved the excitement of Atlantic City. Debbie was known as the quiet, reliable person on the desk. If there was any problem, Debbie could fix it. Never one to eat quickly, Debbie's daily breakfast and lunch would be shared at the entire trading desk.

Debbie's biggest challenge in life was to balance her career and family life, which she did admirably. To her daughters, Danielle 11, and Samantha 5, she was the tutor, track coach, and mommy; to her husband Joe, his lifelong love; to her brothers, sisters, and Mom, the glue that kept them together.

Debbie's big heart and sensitivity will always be missed. She inspired us and we miss her greatly.

Jacqueline Donovan

Jacqueline Donovan, 34, first arrived as a temporary secretary at KBW and with her infectious personality and strong work ethic, was encouraged soon thereafter to work full-time. Jackie quickly made friends throughout the firm. KBW employees of all ages, of varying stature in the firm, male and female, were all drawn to her outgoing and humorous nature. As a KBW employee would pass through the executive area, a visit with Jackie was an obligatory stop.

Outside of work, Jackie maintained a great enthusiasm and generous spirit toward her friends. Her transcendent charm made her great friends with KBW investment bankers, old confidants from Catholic grammar school, and even bikers who revved their deafening motorcycle engines in salute at her memorial mass. As her father, James Donovan said, "These stories make Jackie sound like a party animal. Well, she was."

Jackie grew up in Malverne, New York, and had been living with her grandmother. Jackie also leaves her father, mother, two sisters, and two brothers.

Frank J. Doyle

Frank J. Doyle, 39, was an executive vice president and a member of the board of directors at KBW. A graduate of Bowdoin College, Frank joined KBW in 1985 as an equity trader. He developed an expertise in arbitrage trading and used his skills to create a thriving arbitrage business on KBW's trading desk. In 2000, Frank was promoted to the head of equity trading and was subsequently elected to KBW's board.

Frank was a hockey goaltender at Bowdoin, and continued to play the game throughout his life. He was the consummate athlete, an avid runner, and occasional tri-athlete, always pushing himself and those around him to perform at their best. Whether in or out of the workplace, Frank led by example—an example of hard work, class, loyalty, and respect. Knowing Frank was to know his dry and colorful sense of humor, and his acute insight into people.

More than anything, Frank cherished his family and friends. He always found the time to gather with pals for a "friendly" game of golf, or spend quiet weekends in Quebec with his wife Kimmy and children Zoe and Garrett.

Christopher Michael Duffy

Christopher Michael Duffy, 23, joined KBW's equity trading desk during the summer of 2000, following his graduation from Villanova University. Chris or Duff as he was known to all his friends enjoyed his time on the desk learning from Brad Vadas and Danny McGinley.

His family knew him as the most determined and the best organized. His brothers, Brian and Kevin, knew him as the most competitive. He liked to dress sharp and took great pride in his personal appearance. He loved buying things online, especially for his younger twin sisters, Kara and Caitlin. His friends knew him as the organizer whether it was finding a summer house in the Hamptons or throwing a party at his parents' house.

Chris graduated from Fordham Prep where he played football for four years. He also played lacrosse serving as captain his senior year. This past season the lacrosse team wore his lacrosse and football number "41" on a black patch on their uniforms.

Michael Duffy

Michael Duffy, 29, joined KBW in July 2001 as a salesman in the fixed income department. He was well thought of by coworkers and peers alike. He was on the cusp of success. On September 18, he would have turned 30 years old.

Michael was a beautiful man both inside and out. People were drawn to him like a magnet. He was fortunate enough to have a closely knit circle of friends including eight friends from his high school career. Michael was the glue that kept everyone together.

He organized golf trips for them every year. Michael even planned a trip to Ireland one year. Michael was in five wedding parties last year, including being the best man at his brother John's wedding.

When all his friends were together with his family to celebrate his life, one friend said, "Everyone who knew Michael loved him." Michael wore his heart on his sleeve. All he wanted to do was make everyone happy. He had a wonderful balance of priorities: family, friends, work, and fun....and fun he had! He had done more with his short time than most do in a lifetime. Michael backpacked through Europe for two months after college with one of his closest friends. It was a trip truly cherished.

As his older brother John said in his eulogy, "I have always been proud of Michael. Every time I would meet someone, I would think, 'Wait until they meet my brother.' And when you meet Michael for the first time, I'm sure one's first impression of him is large, athletic stature, natural good looks, and magnetic charisma that immediately tells you—Hey, this guy might be someone special. Then he would come over and give you a Mike Duffy smile, a warm sincere smile. That's when you would be certain that this guy is someone special."

Michael was a native of Long Island where he graduated in 1989 from St. Anthony's High School in South Huntington. He graduated from Manhattan College where he played baseball. He was especially close to his family. He is the son of the late New York District Court Judge John Duffy who died in January 2002, and is survived by his mother Barbara, his brother John, and his sister Mary Kay.

Dean P. Eberling

Dean P. Eberling, 44, was senior vice president in the equity research department at KBW, having joined the firm in March of 2000. He had been in the securities industry since the mid-1980s and worked at several firms including: Merrill Lynch, Lehman

Brothers, and Prudential Securities. Dean had been a top-ranked analyst by the All-American Institutional Investors poll for several years for Securities Brokerage/Asset Management and had also been cited in the *Wall Street Journal* annual survey several times. Dean was a wealth of knowledge, truly dedicated, and took deep pride in his work. He always made a point of sharing his knowledge and mentoring others as he found sincere satisfaction in helping others succeed. While sometimes perceived as serious or "Professor Eberling" as one colleague would fondly refer to him, Dean enjoyed life, loved to laugh, and enjoyed life as a prankster. He made the people around him simply feel happy and his generosity was extraordinary.

Dean was truly a leader to the end. That tragic day when he helped two coworkers from an elevator stuck between floors, he took control of a very dire situation and helped save two lives. For that and so many other positive ways he impacted lives, we are eternally grateful.

Dean is survived by his wife Amy and daughters Cori and Lauren. He was a loving husband and father whose family was the most important people in his life. We miss you terribly and think of you all the time.

Brad Fetchet

Brad Fetchet, 25, joined Keefe, Bruyette & Woods, Inc. in 2000 as a trading assistant and quickly picked up the art of market making as well as understanding bank stocks. After less than one year at KBW, Brad was trading his own pad. Brad graduated from Bucknell where he played lacrosse. Brad was a very bright, refined, and unassuming young man. In a nutshell, he was very "Keefe-like."

Brad was not about the spotlight—a novelty on any Wall Street trading desk. Brad was known as Fetch on the desk because there was already a Brad on the desk, who was many years his senior. Fetch was a breath of fresh air and never thrived on attention.

He was very interested in computers and was a big fan of the Dave Matthews Band. Brad thoroughly enjoyed the friendships he made on the desk and the fun atmosphere we all once bathed in. In addition, he had an unforgettable smile.

Brad is survived by his parents and two younger brothers. He was a rare and beautiful spirit who imbued the world with kindness and light during his short life. We will miss Fetch always.

Jeffery Fox

Jeffery Fox, the chief financial officer of KBW, joined the company in December 2000. Jeff, a native of the New York area, was recruited from his position with First Union in North Carolina to become the third CFO in KBW's history. He was a member of the company's Senior Management Operating Committee.

When he started, Jeff immediately adjusted into KBW's culture. His easy-going style helped him make friends in the company. It was hard to imagine that he had not spent his entire career at KBW. He used his energy and skills to add a new dimension to KBW's accounting and financial operations. He would often come to work on a Monday with a new idea that he had come up with over the weekend. He implemented new budgeting, expense, and capital monitoring techniques and developed a host of reports to make management smarter about our company. He once told his wife Nancy, that his goal was to be the best CFO the company had ever had, and he was well on his way to getting there.

Jeff loved planning to make his house a great home for his family. When he moved to join KBW, he was lucky to find a home on the same street as the one he had sold when he left for North Carolina. Jeff was a family man and the love, pride, and joy he had for his twin daughters, Amanda and Jessica, and his son, Gregory, were easy to see. He had a great marriage and once told a coworker that he and his wife shared everything, including smoking cigars together. He described his wife as his best friend and partner. Everyone he knew misses him every day.

William R. Godshalk

For William R. Godshalk, 35, planning the next vacation was always a top priority. Whether it was a golf weekend with his closest friends at Pinehurst, North Carolina, or a quiet getaway with his fiancée, Aleese Hartmann, to the exclusive Island of St. Barth's, the man from Yardsley, Pennsylvania, relished in arranging his next trip. But what Bill cherished more than the actual planning, was the joy he saw it bring his friends and family.

Bill Godshalk spent six years at KBW as a vice president of equity sales. More than helping his customers understand bank and insurance stocks, Bill took pride in being a very good friend to those who gave him business. There were many weeks in which he spent more time in Philadelphia than in New York, where he was based. For Bill, taking his clients to a ballgame or sending them a bottle of wine for a special occasion was more important than sending them a report by e-mail. Life was good, but it was much better when it was experienced with people he could call friends.

In the summer of 2001, Bill took a major step towards sharing all his moments with a friend. On a warm August night, he asked Aleese to marry him. We are all sure that what Bill cherished most from that moment was the joy he shared with Aleese.

David Graifman

David Graifman, 41, was an equity analyst in the research department, covering the financial guaranty companies as well as the GSEs. Bookish in appearance, and armed with a dry, sarcastic

sense of humor, David was a man of hobbies, a collector of curi-
ous objects and obscure knowledge. David's unique sense of style
was exemplified by his daily selection of watches which he ro-
tated as frequently as others changed neckties. It was hard to
hang around David without learning something, and KBW clients
found David's research and insight valuable. Originally trained as
a credit analyst, David quickly distinguished himself as a stock
picker and a favorite resource of KBW's buy-side clientele. David
was newly married to Christine Huhn and lived on the Upper
East Side of Manhattan. He was extremely family-oriented, particularly close to his nephew, but always found time to root for his
favorite home team, the New York Mets.

Mary Lou Hague

Mary Lou Hague, 26, first came to work for us as a summer intern
in corporate finance in 1995. After graduating from the University of North Carolina and working for Morgan Keegan for two
years, she returned to KBW in 1998. Mary Lou brought tremendous enthusiasm to her job and always had a wonderful smile.
She held her own in corporate finance particularly in support of
the University of North Carolina basketball against the recent
alumni from rival Duke University.

Mary Lou transferred to research in the fall of 2000 and became
a favorite among the New England and Puerto Rican banks she followed. She made some great recommendations for our investing
clients and was so well liked that Western Bank dedicated their list-
ing on the New York Stock Exchange in honor of Mary Lou.

Mary Lou loved New York City, attending rock concerts,
traveling to Europe, and enjoying her many friends. She is greatly
missed by her wonderful family from Parkersburg, West Virginia,
and all of us who were blessed by her warm smile and friendship.

Frances Haros

Fran Haros was a valued employee of KBW for over 20 years. She began as the receptionist and retained that position her entire career. Fran lived in Staten Island and endured a rather long trip to work every day. Never letting the weather stop her. Be it rain, sleet, or snow, Fran made it to work.

Fran's family, her son Nicholas, daughters Andrea and Maria, came first and foremost in her life. Their happiness was of the utmost importance to her. In addition, Fran always went out of her way for her numerous grandchildren.

Fran enjoyed shopping but traveling was what she loved. Every year Fran planned a grand adventure. Her trips would include a friend or family member with whom she could share her experience. Fran's dedication and familiarity will be greatly missed.

Kris Hughes

Kris Hughes, 30, was vice president in equity trading. Kris was a risk arbitrage sales trader at Keefe, Bruyette & Woods, Inc. He was very talented and ambitious, and helped make the arbitrage desk one of the firm's most profitable groups. Kris was also the best dresser on the trading desk.

Kris would also often describe the excitement of trading using the analogy of dating. Kris reveled in finding the natural side of trade. If Kris found a natural seller for his buyer, and got the seller to cancel his working order away to cross stock naturally with him, it was the ultimate thrill. He said it was like bumping into an ex-girlfriend and her new boyfriend at a party and walking away with the woman at the end of the night.

Kris loved a few things: golf, politics, nature, and fly-fishing. Kris is survived by his parents, his sister Elaine, and his brother

Keith, who worked along side Kris at one point in his career. Kris will be deeply missed by us all.

Scott Johnson

Elegant, not only in the physical aspect, although he did have some endearing qualities such as tall, thin, blonde, elongated smile, and very well dressed. But also in thought: Jewish studies at Trinity College.

In word: Research reports at Keefe, Bruyette & Woods, Inc.; just beginning to get his words, his thoughts into print, and his name on the covers, such promise.

In deed: Travels to Egypt, Cuba, Montclair, and Brooklyn.

In friendship: What wonderful friends he had, how they cherished him.

In family: He seemed to look a little like all of them: his father and mother, Tom and Ann, his brother and sister, Tom and Margaret, so caring, so close, so much love.

Donald J. Kauth

Donald J. Kauth, 51, was first employed at First Albany and then Alex Brown but then he joined our research department to cover regional banks in the Northeast and Midwest. He was well regarded and well liked by his banking clients, institutional investors, and fellow analysts. During his time at KBW, he was a valuable mentor to our younger bank analysts.

Don was a devoted father as demonstrated by his return home every weekend to Saratoga Springs to visit with his children. He enjoyed accompanying his children to their soccer and hockey games. His loyalty to his children was always important. He was his daughter, Kathleen's, number one fan; she was captain of the

Brown University women's hockey team. One colleague's last conversation with Don in early September was to congratulate him on Kathleen being named to the U.S. Women's Olympic Hockey Squad. He was smiling and excited, as you would expect.

Don was a good friend to us at KBW, a wonderful father, and number one cheerleader to his children. He will be greatly missed by all.

Karol Keasler

Karol Keasler, 42, was an original. When KBW's event coordinator entered a room, people knew it. Whether it was the different pair of glasses she wore for her different moods, or her girlish, booming voice, Karol was not easily missed. She was a connoisseur of fine food and wine, a world traveler who could always find reason to celebrate—and a fun, festive way to do it—at the drop of a hat. She was perfect for her role at KBW, creating and managing clients' events, and was known, by name and reputation, by many more people than ever had the pleasure of meeting her. In her nearly four years at KBW, she had established herself as someone worth knowing, someone who could always make a moment lighter, and someone who could make just about anything happen. One year when a colleague was celebrating an important birthday, Karol arranged a belly dancer and all cheered who witnessed it. The woman had been a housemate in Karol's Fire Island share.

Nearly everyone has a Karol Keasler story, and Karol had plenty of her own: the years she'd spent living in Africa, the time in high school she waited on Steve McQueen, her annual Fire Island Luau. Karol was constantly searching for the new and different, filling her plate with off-the-path people, places, and things. She was a master at bringing her magic to others. To know Karol was to know her friends, her mother, and her opinion on just about everything. She not only lived life out loud, she lived it at glass-shattering volume and she made no excuses for it. A woman of uncommon beauty, Karol was not content to be known for that—she was constantly working to improve an already rich palette of talents. She was a master baker, a keen photographer, and a wine enthusiast, and seemed determined to continue to broaden her horizons. Karol, who lived in Brooklyn, New York, was engaged to be married. Although she had no children, she told those she worked closest to, "You are my children."

L. Russell Keene

L. Russell Keene, 33, was a vice president of equity analysis covering the electronic securities brokerage industry. He had joined KBW in March of 2000 as part of the brokerage/asset management team under the leadership of Dean Eberling. Prior to joining KBW, Russell worked at Putnam, Lovell, De Guardiola & Thornton, Inc. and Salomon Smith Barney, beginning as a junior analyst at Prudential Securities in 1996. Russell received his MBA in finance from the University of Tampa in 1993. He was known by his coworkers as a hard working, enthusiastic, genuine, the kind person with a huge appetite and southern ways.

Russell, we were so blessed to have had you as part of our team. Thank you for your inspiration and friendship, for you truly are special to us. Our prayers are with your wife Kristen and your young daughter Mazalee.

Lisa King-Johnson

Lisa King-Johnson joined KBW in 1999, where she was vice president of administration and equity research. Her affable, fun-loving personality made her many friends. She was hard working and took great pride in her job.

On May 19, 2001, she married Jim Johnson and resided in Rockaway, New York, with her two beautiful daughters: Jessica, 8 and Katie, 3. She played an active role in her children's daily activities. She was a Girl Scout leader, joined the PTA committee, and organized charitable events at her eldest daughter's school between Katie's dance recitals.

Lisa especially enjoyed taking the girls camping, to the beach, to N' SYNC concerts, and on vacations to Puerto Rico, where her father resides.

She was a valued employee, loving wife, and dedicated mom who will always be missed.

Vanessa Lynn Przybylo Kolpak

Vanessa, 21, embarked on the pursuit of her career at Keefe, Bruyette & Woods, Inc. in August 2001 following a life exemplified by excellence in a diverse array of personal accomplishments. She excelled as a student at Queen of All Saints and the Academy of the Sacred Heart while balancing her life as a Suzuki violinist, an equestrian, and a budding golfer. At St. Ignatius College Prep in Chicago, she was on the National Honor Society and was recognized as a National Merit Scholar. Again, Vanessa matched academic excellence with extra-curriculum activities, placing first in original oratory as a member of the Chicago Catholic Forensic League while participating on the golf and debate teams. Her life of achievement continued at Georgetown University, where she graduated magna cum laude in 2001 while majoring in economics with minors in philosophy and theatre.

For most people, such accomplishments would personify the hallmark of their existence, their life's mark. For Vanessa, they were merely the appendage of her essence, subsumed by a spirit of immeasurable and eternal impact on those who had the blessing of intertwining their lives with hers.

When asked by those interviewing her for a research position at KBW (that was being sought by hundreds of candidates) what she would do if she didn't get the job, she retorted, "I will become a rock star."

Vanessa is survived by her mother, father, a sister, brother, aunt, and many friends.

Jeannine Laverde

Jeannine Laverde, 36, started working for KBW in November 2000, as a new accounts clerk on the trading floor. Her coworkers and everybody who knew her admired her great sense of humor, intelligence, and dedication to her job.

She resided on Staten Island with her mother Dolores and son Christopher. She was a devoted mother and daughter and her family was her world. Jeannine spent all of her spare time taking care of her son, occupying herself with sports and other activities that would benefit Christopher. In addition, she always made it to his games.

Jeannine will always have a special place in our hearts at KBW and she will be sadly missed.

Joseph A. Lenihan

Joseph A. Lenihan, 41, was a key member of KBW's senior management team. He was director of fixed income, and executive vice president, and a member of the board of directors. Joe joined the firm in 1986 in the fixed income group in Hartford, Connecticut, working in the firm's San Francisco office before moving to New York City in 1991 when he took responsibility for managing all of KBW's fixed income relationships. Joe also advised many of the country's largest banking companies with regard to funding and capital raising strategies. Joe also managed the firm's syndicate department. In 2001, Joe was chosen by *Irish American Magazine* as one of the top 50 Irish Americans on Wall Street.

Joe was one of the most loved employees at KBW. He had charisma that could brighten a room and a world-class sense of humor. Joe was talented, knew his business well, and was the consummate team player. Shortly after September 11, an employee at KBW said it best when he said, "Joe Lenihan probably defined the KBW culture better than anyone else."

Joe was born and raised in West Hartford, Connecticut, and received his BS and MBA from the University of Connecticut. He was the youngest of six children. Most recently, Joe lived in Cos Cob, Connecticut, with his wife Ingrid and their three children, Megan, Gabriele, and Joseph. In Cos Cob, Joe was an active participant volunteer in his children's activities. Because of his warm personality, honesty, and outgoing nature, Joe earned the unofficial title of "the mayor of Cos Cob."

Adam Lewis

Adam Lewis was a senior vice president in equity trading. He was a market maker, a proprietary trader, and one of the senior leaders on the desk. Adam grew up in the Bronx, was a star athlete at the Dalton School in Manhattan, and went to Hamilton College, where he also played football.

Adam didn't just live life, he attacked it. He ate more and faster than anyone had ever seen. He would play basketball or flag football on a bad knee that would have kept anyone else on the couch. He had passion in everything he did. His greatest passion was his family. He rushed out of the office daily to make an early train home in order to spend an extra half hour at night with his kids. His priorities were in order. Adam is survived by his wife, Patty, daughters, Reilly, Caroline, Sophie, and son, Sam.

Adam was very important to the desk and we miss him dearly.

Marvin Gavin Ludvigsen

Marvin Gavin Ludvigsen, 32, was a rising star in the KBW fixed income department. In his eight years at KBW, Mark had established himself as one of the top-producing sales professionals in the department. His likeable and engaging personality, dedicated work effort, and intellect were all attributes that contributed to Mark's success. Mark was primarily responsible for accounts in the metro New York and Philadelphia markets. Some of KBW's most important accounts knew "Lud" as an honest, hard working, and insightful salesman.

Always a gentleman, Mark was considerate and generous. Mark's colleagues and seemingly unlimited number of friends knew they could rely on his candid humor to pick up their day. Mark was a passionate rugby player. Starting with intercollegiate competition at William & Mary, he continued honing his skills at the New York Athletic Club after college. Mark's distinguished playing career at the NYAC earned him many accolades including being chosen by his peers as the president of the NYAC Rugby Club.

Mark and his wife of three years, Maureen Kelly, made their home in New York City. Born in South Africa, Mark was raised in Pottersville, New Jersey, and graduated from William & Mary College.

Sean Lugano

Sean Lugano, 28, was an associate sales trader on the equity trading desk. Sean joined KBW in 2000. Always a hard worker, Sean was constantly the first to answer the phone. He brought new meaning to the word hustle.

Sean liked his nights, too. Sleep was not a priority. He was part owner of two bars: Opal and Rathbone's and we would joke that KBW was his hobby. Never shy, Sean would raise his eyebrow, tilt his head, smirk, and call himself Mel Gibson. Sean was an excellent athlete who was also involved in rugby and played on a team with two other KBW employees.

Sean loved his family. His survivors include his mother, two brothers, two sisters, and two nieces, Katie Sean and Emma Sean, both born after September 11. Every Sunday, Sean would join his family at John's Pizza after Mass. He never once missed that tradition. We miss Sean dearly.

Michael P. McDonnell

Michael P. McDonnell, 34, was a senior vice president and controller/director of accounting. He attended Stony Brook University as an undergraduate and during his five years at KBW he completed his MBA at Barauch College. We knew Mike as the jack-of-all-trades. His vast knowledge and understanding of the financial industry made it easy for him to relate information to us in a comprehensive manner.

Mike's sense of humor is what we most remember him for. Whenever the stress of the job started to accumulate, he would always smile and say his favorite phrase: "I love this job!" Mike's laid back personality made it easy to work with him. He was a great leader and was well liked, admired, and respected by all his peers and employees.

Mike loved his family dearly. He was a proud dad of two sons: Kevin and Brian. He was also a wonderful husband to his wife of eight years, Cheryl McDonnell. In addition, he was a big sports fan. He enjoyed talking about the Jets and Mets especially when he attended the games.

Mike will be remembered for the enthusiasm he had for life. He is missed greatly and will always be in our hearts.

Dan McGinley

Dan McGinley, 40, was a senior vice president in equity trading who joined KBW in 1993. Dan made markets in New England banks and New York thrifts. He was an integral part of the desk and always kept the mood light.

Danny, a seminary student turned trader, could trade a stock, crack a joke, and sing a song all in one minute. He was great at impersonations. Danny loved life and lived it by the golden rule. He loved hockey and played with the boys every week. As his brother said at his memorial service, "Dan worked his entire life to get to where he is now."

Danny is survived by his wife, Peggy, and his five children: Terrance, Maddie, Peter, Annie, and Patrick. We will miss Danny always.

Lindsay Morehouse

Bob Stapleton had the privilege of knowing Lindsay, 24, all her life because she was the only child of his sister Kathy Maycen. She grew up in Florida, became a great tennis player at a young age, but chose to come north for prep school and college because she was also a hard-working student with ambition. She was captain of her tennis teams at St. Paul's School and Williams College where she received All-American recognition and played for the NCA Division III Championship her junior year.

When Lindsay graduated from college in 2000, she went to work for a small investment bank in Virginia but soon wanted the faster pace of New York. She joined KBW in April 2001 and started working directly for Tom Theurkauf, our All-American bank analyst. Under Tom's tutelage, Lindsay became an accomplished junior analyst and by summer she was writing her own research reports.

After work, Lindsay would organize her friends for parties and rock concerts, particularly a band called "Seeking Homer." She also found time for volunteer work and had just been accepted into the Big Sister program in New York.

Lindsay accomplished a great deal in her young life and was the pride and joy of her loving mom who was blessed to have such a wonderful daughter.

Stephen V. Mulderry

Stephen V. Mulderry, 33, was a vice president on the equity trading desk. He started at KBW in 1997, quickly rising through the ranks and eventually covered some of the firm's best accounts. Many of KBW's most labor-intensive accounts, relied on Stephen's thorough attention. He was a huge asset to the trading desk.

Stephen's quick wit and friendly nature were the marks of his inclusive sense of amiability. He would laugh in disbelief about how much fun we all had at work and questioned if this was even work at all. His brother said Stephen had four passions: family, friends, work, and basketball. His positive energy largely contributed to the unique and wonderful chemistry that was enjoyed on the trading desk at Keefe, Bruyette & Woods, Inc. He graduated from the University of Albany as an All-American Division III basketball player. The sixth of eight children, Stephen was someone who squeezed every ounce out of every day.

Stephen had the ability to light people up inside and had a generosity of spirit that could not go unnoticed and will never be forgotten. We will miss Stephen dearly.

Christopher W. Murphy

Christopher W. Murphy was a senior research analyst at KBW, as well as an attorney, and an accomplished offshore sailor. A native of Connecticut, Chris graduated form Yale University where he was the captain of the sailing team. After leaving Yale, Chris raced a 40-foot sailboat across the Atlantic. In addition, he was the captain and instructor for Sail Caribbean's program for teenage boys and girls. In 1992, Chris received his doctorate with honors from Emory University and went into private practice in Stamford, Connecticut. In 1994, he and his wife, Catherine, moved to Richmond, Virginia, where Chris continued to practice law until he left to attend business school. After earning his MBA from William and Mary, Chris joined Wheat First Securities where he worked as a banking industry research analyst. Chris joined KBW in April 2001.

Chris was known for having an easygoing and egoless nature and an uncanny way of putting others at ease. He was never quick to judge and accepted others as he found them. Chris simply believed in constancy as a friend, father, husband, son, brother, and colleague.

Chris and Catherine lived in Easton, Maryland, with their two beautiful daughters: Hopewell (Hope) and Hannah. For us, Chris was always a fair, warm wind on our beam. We miss him dearly.

Keith O'Connor

Keith O'Connor, 28, was a big man with an even bigger heart.

Keith came to KBW, from Lehman Brothers in 1999 as a 26-year-old assistant trader on the fixed income desk and quickly developed into a valued asset not only in trading but also in working with KBW clients on a daily basis.

Standing an intimidating 6'5" and 250+ pounds, Keith was one of the gentlest people you could ever meet. He had a way about him that could make anyone laugh, especially with his deep knowledge of government and MBS bonds, and his ability to name every song ever played since the 1970s, a feat that has not been duplicated. This is the same man who grew up in Hell's Kitchen, New York City, playing not only basketball with his friends but also the bagpipes as a member of the St. Columcille United Gaelic Pipe throughout his childhood.

Keith's time outside KBW was spent living in Hoboken, New Jersey, with his two most prized possessions: his wife, Sandra and two-year-old daughter, Rhiannon.

Although he only worked at KBW a few short years, his presence will be missed by all that knew him. The Gentle Giant will never be forgotten.

Marni Pont O'Doherty

Marni Pont O'Doherty, 31, was a senior research analyst at KBW and one of the most liked people at the firm. During her six years at KBW, she moved from junior analyst assisting the director of research to one of the most recognized bank analysts on Wall Street; Marni was the gold standard for KBW research. Following southeast institutions including some of the biggest banks in the country, she was a constant, top-tier presence, and a valued analyst. Clients and colleagues alike could always count on a reasoned analysis and an artfully turned phrase. In an industry of unpredictable developments and late-breaking news, Marni was seldom surprised and never unprepared, able to react immediately with more background and insight than one would've thought possible in such short order.

Despite the tireless efforts and hard work that made her the department's rising star, she remained the keeper of the firm's decades-long database and the author of many of KBW's flagships products, well after her responsibilities as a senior analyst made carrying that torch discretionary. She was also known to spend Sunday evenings—between financial modeling and preparing for bank earnings—baking zucchini bread for the sales desk with vegetables from her own garden. She was quick-witted and smart, admired by clients and bank managers alike, and had an unparalleled level of intellectual integrity that kept her work honest and beyond reproach. Everyone who dealt with Marni respected her whether they agreed with her or not, and she combined ambition with ability, which is perhaps the hallmark of success. Marni lived in Armonk, New York, with her husband Joe, in the house of her dreams and a garden that, not unlike Marni, was fast on its way to greatness.

Philip Ognibene

Philip Ognibene, 39, was an assistant market maker on the equity trading desk. He worked at KBW for 16 years. Known to his family as Woody and his friends at KBW as Eddie, he was the heartbeat of both. He always had a smile on his face, and he brought life to any situation.

Hearing him say: "Sons, you gotta taste my mother's sauce!" still rings through our heads. A New Yorker through and through, he loved his Yankees and Islanders. Eddie's mood was tied to the success of the Yankees. He was the kid from the neighborhood who made it to Wall Street. He lived for family gatherings and wiffleball games with his nieces and nephews. Eddie is survived by his mother, father, brother, Blaise, and two sisters, Esther and Anna.

Eddie was simply the heart of the desk.

Cira Patti

Cira M. Patti, 40, who was an administrative assistant for KBW's equity sales desk, was never, ever at a loss for words. Working among the most chatty and verbally adept members of institutional sales, Cira's one-line responses were well renowned, and she often surprised her colleagues with her sarcasm and quick comebacks. Known to challenge anyone with her own opinions, whether it regarded sports or life, Cira was always correct in any squabble. This made her one of the most popular people on the desk.

Cira had her own terms with which she took on the world including frequent trips with friends to the beach house she owned on the Jersey Shore, and late night cocktailing with the girls on Thursday. She even brought her own skim milk to the bars so the bartender could make her White Russians, light.

Cira was also very verbally adept when discussing her family. She talked fondly of her young nieces and nephews, who brought a twinkle to her eye. She was not afraid to show how worried she was for her brother, when he was seriously injured in an accident from which he managed to fully recover. Cira talked of her parents frequently, making sure everyone knew that she would eat only her own family's pasta sauce; everything else was a cheap imitation. An avid sports fan, Cira loved to talk about her Yankees and Giants, two teams she chose to root for if only to spite her father and brother, avid Mets and Jets fans.

Mike Pescherine

Mike Pescherine, 32, joined KBW in 1998 where he covered financial institutions as a salesman in the fixed income department. His easygoing style, integrity, and market knowledge allowed him to develop deep client relationships that extended beyond the workplace. Clients became friends.

Family and friends were the center of Mike's life. So much so that he and his wife Lynn lived in the same New York City apartment building as his brother Tom and his family. Mike looked forward to those nights when he and his wife would babysit for his brother's children. He was also looking forward to starting his own family as he and Lynn had learned in the summer of 2001 that they were expecting their first child. Ryan Michael was born in February 2002.

An everyday man, Mike, or Pesch to his friends, had the knack of making the difficult appear easy. His humility downplayed his many accomplishments. A devoted Penn State graduate, Mike never got tired of talking about Nittany Lions football. He was an accomplished athlete himself, but was unable to play football because of back problems. However, that didn't keep him from wrestling and playing baseball in high school. And once he put his mind to something he would not be deterred as evidenced by his finishing the 1999 and 2000 New York City marathons with his wife.

A New Jersey native, Mike graduated with honors from Parsippany High School and received his BA from Penn State University where he graduated summa cum laude. He also received his MBA from Penn State University, again with honors.

Mike is survived by his wife Lynn; his son Ryan Michael; his parents Thomas and Anne; his three brothers Tom, David, and Bill; his sister Nancy Gionco; and seven nieces and nephews.

Jim Reilly

Jim Reilly, 25, was a bond trader at KBW on the 89th floor. For his age, Jim had a surprising command of the corporate bond market. He quite often could be found at his desk quietly studying banks and spreads late into the evening. Over his short career, Jim had developed a surprisingly large number of relationships across Wall Street. His advice was trusted by both his clients and his colleagues.

Jim, to quote Father O'Brien's remarks at Jim's memorial service, always took his responsibilities very seriously but never took himself very seriously. Jim, as his roommates will confirm, had a robust social life. His ability to balance work and play was a natural gift. Jim grew up in Huntington, Long Island, as the youngest of five brothers and sisters. Tom, Jeanne, and Chris will all tell you that Jim was the favorite. Jim was a natural story teller, athlete, and friend.

Jim earned his BS from William & Mary University. He also studied for a semester at the London School of Economics. Jim is survived by his father, his mother, his brothers and sisters, and his girlfriend Jen.

Joseph Roberto

Joseph Roberto served as vice president for the equity research department and was an outstanding analyst. He covered banks and thrifts in the Midwest United States and Canada. His writings and many publications were stylish, accurate, thorough, and objective. Joe was dedicated to his profession and always conducted himself with integrity and pride. Joe enhanced the reputation of KBW and was an important resource for newspapers and trade publications. Joe's life priorities were in proper order: family, business, and fun. He loved his wife Janet who was his best friend. Joe was a very proud father and a caring and compassionate man involved in social issues and good causes. Joe Roberto was proud to be an American. He lived in New Jersey with his wife Jane and son Joseph Paul.

Joe was born in 1964 in the Bronx and was the older brother to Lorraine and Robert. He attended Clarkstown High School and graduated in 1982. Joe was an honor student who studied at Fordham University and earned a Bachelor of Science in Business Administration in 1986. Also at Fordham, he earned a Master of Business Administration in Finance in 1990. Joe was a huge talent in the complex world of finance.

Joe's favorite holiday was Christmas. Joe loved his beer, tunes, house, and motorcycling. He enjoyed dancing, trips to civil war battlefields, visiting the Bronx Zoo, and coin collecting. Joe Roberto touched us all. We love you, Joe, and have you in our hearts.

Ronald Ruben

Ron Ruben, 35, was a recent addition to KBW's sales trading effort and had been a client of the firm for seven years. His unique experience on both sides of Wall Street made him an adept trader and a favorite of his clients. When Ron Ruben smiled, it beamed through the room like a universal truth. Ron was incorrigibly positive, someone who seemingly couldn't be unhappy. As a member of the New York trading desk, Ron had been with the firm only five months, but in short order he had distinguished himself as a helping hand, a favorite of clients, and the desk's mouthpiece for some of the world's corniest jokes. A client who had known him for years described how every morning Ron would call him up, usually before 8 A.M., and tell him the worst joke he had ever heard—and a completely new one every day, each worst than the last. A KBW colleague remembered setting Ron up at the Museum of Natural History, where, as they passed a large stuffed elephant, he stopped, looked at his date and exclaimed, "Wait! I forgot something in the trunk!" There was no joke too silly and no pun too obvious, but anyone in earshot of a Ron Ruben zinger would be left in stitches. Perhaps even more than for his infamous jokes, Ron was known for helping others. He could be found, at any given moment, doing something for someone else. The weekend before September 11, Ron had helped refinish the floors in the apartment of one of his deskmates. As she later put it, "Ron offered to help, but for Ron that meant actually doing it." Ron adored children, especially his nieces and nephew, and was close with his two sisters. He was a smart, solid person, "one of the good guys," as his sister Leslie put it, and KBW was a better place for knowing him.

John J. Ryan

John J. Ryan, 45, was a senior vice president in equity trading. He was a senior sales trader who assisted in training practically every sales trader at Keefe, Bruyette & Woods, Inc. He taught us to do it the right way. John's brother and father were sales traders on Wall Street as well. It was in their blood. John attended Xavier High School in Manhattan and went to The College of the Holy Cross, where he played football.

John was a prankster. He always drew cartoons of the latest funny event on the desk. He would yell out "war department!" whenever anyone's wife called. But John kept it interesting—he was a man who had a great deal of depth to him.

John loved his family. He was constantly draw up new basketball plays or starting lineups for his kids' softball and basketball games. John is survived by his wife, Patty, and his three children Laura, Collin, and Kristin. We will miss John Ryan always.

Muriel Siskopoulos

Muriel Siskopoulos, 60, joined KBW in 1991 and quickly became friends with several coworkers. She enjoyed working at KBW and everyone who knew her and worked with her admired her friendly, outgoing, and stylish personality.

Muriel lived in Brooklyn with her husband Mark and spent her spare time with her four children: T.J., Terry, Donna, Laura, and two grandchildren. Her favorite pastimes were traveling and shopping (particularly for shoes and clothes). We like to think of Muriel in the hereafter as running a boutique, beautifully dressed with her shoes matching her outfit and always smiling.

Muriel was an asset to the research department at KBW and will always be remembered and missed.

Paul Sloan

Paul Sloan, 26, was an associate in the equity research depart-ment. Prior to moving to New York City in 2000, he worked for the investment firms Morgan-Walke Associates and Sutro & Co. in San Francisco. He attended San Marin High School and Brown University and graduated with a degree in history in 1997. In high school, he achieved All League and All-Bay Area honors as one of the top linemen in Northern California and was also a Na-tional Football Scholar-Athlete Award winner. At Brown, he con-tinued to play football and started for two years as an offensive guard for the Ivy League team. Paul was known by his friends to be driven, enthusiastic, and sweet. In addition, he was a very ded-icated friend and family person as exemplified by his display of pictures of friends, family, and football.

He is survived by his parents, Ron and Muffy Sloan, two brothers, Matt and Peter, and a sister and brother-in-law, Sarah and William Funk. Our thoughts and prayers are with his family.

Greg Spagnoletti

Greg Spagnoletti, 32, joined KBW as a vice president in 1999 where he covered financial institutions as a salesman in the fixed income department. He was highly regarded by his clients as a trustworthy and knowledgeable professional. Many of these rela-tionships went beyond business as Greg built lasting relationships as well.

Greg was truly a New Yorker, having lived in Manhattan for nine years. To work on Wall Street was Greg's dream. He fre-quently told people "I love my job. I get up every morning and I look forward to going into the office. I am so lucky." When anyone ever asked him what he did for a living, Greg would reply: "I work on Wall Street . . . in the World Trade Center." This was said as a matter of pride not arrogance. He never forgot his roots. From Waterbury to Wall Street—Greg made it!

Growing up the third of four boys, Greg was passionate about his family, friends, and hockey. His brothers were his best friends. He always enjoyed recounting the childhood adventures of the four Spagnoletti boys. Known as "Spags," he was meticulous in whatever he did and he was an impeccable dresser. His brother Paul told how he looked forward to getting Greg's hand-me-downs; they were always in great condition. Constantly on the go, Greg could be found checking in on his family, organizing an ice hockey team at Chelsea Piers, or dropping in on the neighborhood merchants with a smile and a story.

A Connecticut native, Greg was a graduate of Watertown High School and Curry College in Milton, Massachusetts, where he attended on an ice hockey scholarship. He loved the outdoors where he enjoyed golf, sailing, hiking, and cycling.

Greg leaves his parents Richard and Maria; three brothers: Mark, Chris, and Paul; and his long time girlfriend Gretchen Zurn.

Derek Statkevicus

Derek Statkevicus, 31, was an analyst in the equity research department following bank stocks having worked under the mentorship of David Berry, KBW's director of research for a few years. Derek graduated from Ithaca College in 1993. Derek will always be remembered as a fun-loving and outgoing individual with a very distinctive voice and laughter. He was a hard-worker, a good friend, a caring father, and a loving husband. He is survived by his wife Kimberley, two-year-old Tyler, and his second son Derek Chase, who was born in January after the tragedy. Derek beamed when he spoke of his family. Colleagues remember his desk being surrounded by pictures of his loved ones. May God bless his family and keep them safe always and help them heal.

Craig W. Staub

Craig W. Staub, 30, was vice president of trading for KBW. He joined KBW in 1992 as an equity salesman covering New York area and United Kingdom accounts. Craig left the firm in 1994 to join Langdon Street Capital as an analyst and trader. Later he became a partner. In 1998, Craig rejoined KBW as an analyst in the asset management group and then switched to become a position trader at the broker-dealer.

Craig was born and raised in the Bronx, attended high school at the Bronx High School of Science and graduated with a BS in Business Administration as summa cum laude from Boston University. Craig had a great intellect, an unrelenting curiosity, and a desire to discover great companies. In addition, he possessed a friendly outgoing demeanor that made you always feel welcome.

Craig and his wife Stacey had recently moved from New York City to Basking Ridge, New Jersey, where they had built a home. September 22 would have been Craig's birthday and his wife, Stacey gave birth to a baby girl—Juliette Craig Staub. Craig's family and friends were very important to him. We will miss him greatly.

Derek Sword

Derek Sword, 29, was born in Dundee, Scotland. Derek and his twin brother, Alan, were Scottish Junior Champions at tennis doubles.

Following graduation, he began to work as a buy side analyst at a small investment bank in Glasgow, Scotland. In 1995, Derek was recruited by Keefe, Bruyette & Woods, Inc. to manage European accounts for the institutional sales desk. Eventually, he broadened his account base to include domestic clients as well. Derek began his career as an associate and was successively promoted to assistant vice president and finally vice president.

Derek possessed a most witty and fun-loving personality but was serious when it came to work matters. He would often travel back and forth to Europe several times in a given month. Derek will be remembered for his contributions to the "Wall of Shame" which he and Bill Godshalk cared for diligently. Derek was an expatriate living in New York City, however, from day one he was one of us; whether "us" meant his friends and colleagues at KBW, his clients, his colleagues, and teammates from the NYAC squash team or just one of his peers. He was and always will be the "Swordsman."

Derek is survived by his fiancée Maureen Sullivan, who he planned to marry in 2002, his twin brother Alan, his older brother Graham, and his parents.

Kevin Szocik

Kevin Szocik, 27, made a "big" impression whether he was on a trading floor addressing the KBW salesforce with his latest stock idea or quarterbacking the Fordham University football team as its captain.

Physical stature was only part of the equation and his competitiveness epitomized Kevin, according to his younger brother Brendan. Kevin wasn't satisfied as a successful three-sport athlete in high school or Patriot League Academic All-Conference Athlete. A voracious competitor, Kevin needed to excel at everything in life whether it was golf, boating, fishing, diving, snowmobiling, or as a bank stock analyst on Wall Street. Kevin picked the right occupation for a competitor. When he changed the rating on a stock based on the strength of his convictions, he often caused the prices of the New York thrift stocks he covered to gyrate.

Lorraine, Kevin's wife, would probably prefer to remember the softer side of her husband whom she met as a freshman at Fordham University; she spent frequent weekends with the McNeill family enjoying summers on eastern Long Island.

Kevin was raised a Patriots and Red Sox fan in Lunenburg, Massachusetts, by his parents Tom and Sheila. Kevin's older sister Lisa has fond memories of Kevin vacationing at the family cabin on a quiet lake in Maine.

No matter how quiet the family weekends with loved ones got during the summer, you could always count on Kevin to liven things up. Kevin's lovable composure would inevitably break down into a whirlwind explosion of horrific swear words, golf clubs, shoes, clothes, or anything not nailed down when on those rare occasions he missed his mark. Ninety-nine percent of the time, the family enjoyed Kevin's successes and the remainder of the time they sat back and enjoyed the show.

Thomas Francis Theurkauf Jr.

Thomas Francis Theurkauf Jr. was executive vice president and a member of the board of directors at KBW since 2000. He was also associate director of research and followed an eclectic set of banks and thrifts ranging from the super-regional banks in the northeast to the thrifts in the western United States. Tom was frequently a guest on CNBC and was often quoted in the *Wall Street Journal, New York Times,* and other business publications. His many accomplishments included recently being named the top bank analyst in the country by the *Wall Street Journal.*

Tom was born and raised in Glastonbury, Connecticut, and received a BS from MIT and an MBA from Dartmouth's Amos Tuck School. Tom was a delight to work with and a huge asset to the firm. Tom had boundless energy, an incredibly upbeat demeanor, a constant smile, and a "can do" approach to life. Clients and top managements loved working with Tom.

Tom, his wife Robin, and their three boys—Thomas Francis (Tommy), Edward Arthur (Teddy), and Charles Henry (Henry)—lived in Stamford, Connecticut. He loved to plan weekends with Robin, fish and play with the boys, and entertain friends and family. Tom was an avid runner and always took time to help others. We will miss him terribly.

Eric R. Thorpe

Eric R. Thorpe, 35, was an institutional equity salesman for KBW. Affectionately known as Rick, he worked at KBW for nine years where he was a dedicated professional. Many of Rick's clients adored him for his knowledge and understanding of the daily markets, as well as his quick wit and spirited personality. He dealt with the most sophisticated investors on Wall Street and was their most dependable advisor.

Rick's coworkers were constantly entertained by his humorous comments and frequent razzing. He was always approachable and immediately personable with all whom he met. It was almost a guarantee that after your first meeting with Rick, you would receive a nickname that would be used by all at KBW. Rick's outgoing personality positively affected everyone with whom he came into contact.

But to discuss Rick in only these terms would be to deny the true focus of his being. Rick was a family man first and foremost, dedicated to the life he shared with his wife Linda, and 16-month-old daughter Alexis. He rushed home at the end of the day for an extra few minutes of time with his two favorite people. Writing in a journal, Rick described his life best. "Linda and Alexis have made my life complete. I don't need anything else. I spend my day trading stocks, trying to make money but it's the women closest to me that have put true purpose in my existence." That more than anything else reflects the true Rick Thorpe, devoting his life to the ones he loved.

Nichola A. Thorpe

Nichola A. Thorpe, 22, was an accounts payable representative for KBW. She was a very ambitious person and this was exemplified by her working full-time to fund her education at Berkeley College to complete her degree in accounting. Nichola was a dedicated and hard-working individual who was determined to succeed in whatever she did.

Many saw Nichola as a very shy and soft-spoken individual. Those who knew her appreciated the strong-willed, funny, kindhearted, and intelligent person that she was. Being of Jamaican descent, Nichola was very proud of her heritage and expressed it in the music she enjoyed as well as the social events she attended.

Nichola had just completed her first year at KBW. She was one month shy of her 23rd birthday. She is missed terribly by her family and friends and will forever be in our hearts.

Gregory J. Trost

Gregory J. Trost, 26, was an associate analyst in the equity research department at KBW having joined the firm in March 2000 as part of the brokerage/asset management team. Greg, who would have turned 27 years old on St. Patrick's Day, was a 1997 graduate from William and Mary where he earned a BBA in finance. He had successfully completed his Level II CFA. Greg was known to his family and friends for his kindness, generosity, and love of life and was equally famous for his glowing personality and sense of humor. He was extremely animated and could light up a room with his laughter and smiles. He is remembered by his coworkers as being a very bright, hard-working, dedicated individual and we feel so fortunate to have had him as part of our team.

Greg's parents and sister live in New York City on the Upper East Side just blocks from where Greg had lived. Our thoughts and prayers remain with the family always and we hope that they find peace in knowing what a special person their son Greg was to so many.

Brad Vadas

Brad Vadas, 37, was a senior vice president in equity trading. He started in 1986 and was a market maker and proprietary trader. Brad was a very important part of our desk. Brad grew up in Weston, Connecticut, and went to Boston College. Like many others, KBW was his only job.

Brad was a great trader. In fact, he was good at almost everything he did. He was the most competitive person many of us had ever met. He loved to sing and was a great dancer. He really enjoyed sports and played softball almost every weekend. Weekends in Connecticut were very important to him, back where he grew up and away from the hustle and bustle of the city. Brad is survived by his parents, his brother, and his sister.

Brad was a friend and will be missed.

Joseph Visciano

Joseph Visciano, 22, joined KBW in the summer of 2001. He had just graduated from Boston College, magna cum laude, with a degree in finance and had expressed interest in getting an MBA. He started out on the trading desk, and was to rotate throughout each department of the firm before he settled into a particular area.

Joe liked trading and the environment on the desk so much that he had his sights set on ultimately becoming a trader at the firm. He was a very bright and eager young man, serious about his job, and determined to do very well in his career. Even during the slow summer trading days, Joe would read through Keefe, Bruyette & Woods, Inc. research. He was a sponge and didn't have a lazy bone in his body.

Joe is survived by his parents and younger brother Jason. Although Joe only worked at Keefe, Bruyette & Woods, Inc. for six weeks, he made his mark on all of us.

Jean Marie Wallendorf

Jean Marie Wallendorf, 23, started working at KBW in March of 2001, as a new accounts clerk on the trading floor. She was a hard-working, bright, and beautiful young lady with her whole life ahead of her. She had a warm and friendly smile, easy going personality, and everyone got along with her.

As a child, Jean Marie lived in Florida with her mother, step-father, and four younger siblings. Jean Marie came to New York mainly for the lifestyle. She fell in love with her boyfriend Joe and lived with him in Brooklyn. She was the oldest child, and she genuinely adored her younger siblings, especially her two youngest brothers mainly because she watched her mother give birth to them. Her family meant the world to her; her mother was her best friend.

Jean Marie will always have a special place in our hearts and will never be forgotten.

James T. Waters

James T. Waters Jr., 39, joined KBW in 1997. He served as senior vice president of the fixed income division and specialized in trading and sales of mortgage-backed securities. He was frequently quoted by the Bloomberg news service and provided excellent commentary on economic data and current events.

Known as Muddy to his friends and colleagues, he had many interests. He enjoyed politics, golf, finance, economics, and reading. He loved going out to the Hamptons and socializing with friends. One of the highlights of his life was attending George W. Bush's inauguration. Upon his return to the office, he proudly shared his photographs of prominent political figures.

He was wise beyond his years and his qualities of character and integrity were admired by all. Muddy was a compassionate man and willingly helped family, friends, and colleagues.

Muddy was born in Danbury, Connecticut, and grew up in Litchfield. He was a graduate of George Washington University. He was single and lived on the Upper East Side in Manhattan. He left his mother, Joanne Waters, his sister Karen, and brother Chris, too soon. Muddy will live within our hearts forever.

David Winton

David Winton was born and raised in Weathersfield, Connecticut, and attended Weathersfield High School. He graduated from Fordham University, College of Business Administration in 1994. While at Fordham, he was an honor student, a member of the Globe program, studied at University College, London, England, and was CFO of the student-run Fordham Federal Credit Union. At graduation, he received the CBA Alumni Association Award.

After graduation, David took a job with Chase Manhattan Bank. Despite making many close friends there, David left Chase to join Keefe, Bruyette & Woods' equity research department in 1995. He was initially responsible in assisting Tom Theurkauf, a senior equity analyst at KBW. However, David's insightful research enabled him to gain his own coverage at a relatively young age. Prior to September 11, David had primary responsibility over west coast banks and thrifts and was the vice president of the equity research department. Dave continued his studies while employed at KBW and became a Chartered Financial Analyst. He was also a member of the New York Society of Security Analysts.

Dave had many interests: He was an avid skier, a history buff, played golf, and loved a good game of poker and volleyball. He was devoted to his mom and sister, was a loyal friend with a quick wit, and had a host of friends across the country. Dave was to marry his fiancée Amy Lane on November 17, 2001.

David is survived by his sister Sara Elizabeth Winton, his mother Joan Wise Winton, and his fiancée Amy Lane.

Brent Woodall

Brent Woodall, 31, a vice president sales-trader joined the equity trading desk at KBW in 1996. In addition to sales trading, Brent was also a market maker in many of the thrift conversions. Brent graduated from Cal Berkeley where he played football and baseball. He played minor league baseball before joining KBW.

Brent was extremely intelligent and always demanded excellent execution. If Brent had any problems with the floor brokers, watch out—Brent was not afraid to bang phones. He broke more than four phones during his years at KBW.

Brent married Tracy Pierce in August of 2000. Many people from work flew out to their wedding in Las Vegas. Brent was a big and fierce competitor but he was a teddy bear on the inside. He was caught pouring over his registry on the Internet on more than one occasion. Brent learned he and Tracy were expecting a baby shortly before September 11.

Brent is survived by his wife Tracy, daughter Pierce Ashley, his parents, his brother Craig, and sister Erin.

Richard Woodwell

Richard Woodwell, 44, was a senior vice president on the equity trading desk. He was known to all as Woody. No other name was needed. Woody loved markets and used his skills in covering KBW's west coast accounts as well as making markets in the west coast bank stocks. He also enjoyed options trading and enlightened his colleagues on the virtues of selling premiums.

He had a very popular personality and always enjoyed the moment. His healthy approach to life was the envy of all. He lived life to the fullest. He loved playing golf in beautiful places, drinking the finest cabernets, and savoring an occasional cigar. Possessed with a wry wit, Woody was always on the guest list for any party or outing. He kept life and its meaning in perspective as the biggest joy in his life was his family. He is survived by his wife Linda and three children: Richard (11), Margaret (9), and Eleanor (4).

John Bentley Works

John Bentley Works, 36, rejoined KBW as a proprietary equity trader in March of 2001. John had finally embarked on his dream job, trading stocks. Many of the same colleagues with whom John had started 15 years earlier at KBW welcomed him back in his new role. He started as an equity research analyst at KBW in 1986, and in 1990, accepted a job as the fixed income credit analyst. Always seeking new challenges, John left KBW in 1992 to join J.P. Morgan's bond department where he subsequently rose to the role of fixed income strategist. In each of these job moves, John had been approached as the "best candidate for the job." He was widely acknowledged as the "brightest person I knew" by friends and colleagues.

John was blessed with an incredible thirst for information and an even more incredible ability to understand and retain it. He read constantly, and no topic was off-limits. John was also a skilled and engaging conversationalist, often conversing for hours on almost any subject. In his personal and professional life, both JP Morgan and KBW, John always had an audience.

John was raised in Rowayton, Connecticut, and graduated from Middlebury College with a double major in German and Economics. An avid sailor, John enjoyed long cruises on his 25-foot sailboat in Long Island Sound.

John and his wife Pam, with their daughter Allison, had just moved from New York City to the coast of Connecticut in May 2001.

INDEX